World Religions and Beliefs

Mystics
AND
Psychics

World Religions and Beliefs

Mystics AND Psychics

Joanne Mattern

MORGAN REYNOLDS
PUBLISHING

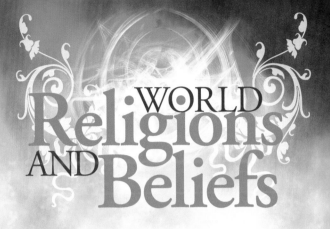

WORLD
Religions
AND Beliefs

Founders of Faiths

Mystics and Psychics

The Birth of Christianity

The Birth of Islam

World Religions and Beliefs: Mystics and Psychics

Copyright © 2012 by Morgan Reynolds Publishing

Library of Congress Cataloging-in-Publication Data

Mattern, Joanne, 1963-
Mystics and psychics / by Joanne Mattern.
    p. cm. -- (World religions and beliefs)
Includes bibliographical references and index.
ISBN 978-1-59935-148-3
1. Psychics--Biography--Juvenile literature. 2. Mystics--Biography--
Juvenile literature. I. Title.
 BF1026.M38 2011
 133.8092'2--dc22
 [B]

                                                      2010008690

Printed in the United States of America
First Edition

For my husband, Jim, another fan of the mysterious

Contents

Introduction
Knowing the Unknown

What will happen tomorrow? Twenty years from now? What does fate have in store for us? To constantly look toward the future is very much human nature. In the course of any day, people are thinking about the next instant, the next hour, the next day. American philosopher and essayist Ralph Waldo Emerson once wrote, "If a man carefully examines his thoughts, he will be surprised to find how much he lives in the future."

Though it is impossible to know the future, that has never stopped people from imagining it, or trying to plan for it. That's why horoscopes are so popular, and why throughout history people have consulted sibyls, palm readers, psychics, tarot card readers, soothsayers, shamans, religious prophets, and the like. We have always wanted to see into the future, to know the unknown, to predict the unpredictable. And because this desire to know what might happen is so strong, there has always been a place in history for mystics and psychics.

Mystics and psychics claim to have supernatural powers. Some believe they are born with their powers, while others credit a spiritual source. Still others report receiving their powers after an illness or an accident. There are many different kinds of psychic powers, according to believers in the phenomena. Some of the most common are predicting the future (precognition), knowing what other people are thinking (mental telepathy), or communicating with the dead. Some mystics perform apparent miracles, such as healing the sick. Still others exhibit physical signs of mystic powers, such as having marks called stigmata appear on their hands and feet.

In ancient times, many cultures relied on psychics to foretell the future. In Rome around 1200 BCE, women called sibyls wrote and spoke of the future. During this era, ancient Greece had a prophet known as the Oracle of Delphi. Like the sibyls, the oracle answered questions and made pronouncements about what the future held. The Mayan people, who lived in Mexico and Central America between 250 and 900 CE, relied on astrologers and priests who performed special rituals to predict the future.

Mystics have long been associated with religious traditions. The histories of Muslims, Christians, and Jews are filled with stories of prophets who spoke directly to God or another higher power and received special gifts, such as healing, the ability to be in two places at once, or the ability to know the future. Native American cultures also featured mystics. These mystics were often called shamans or medicine men. They were considered holy people who communicated with the Great Spirit and used their powers to guide and help people on Earth.

Although ancient societies often honored or worshiped people with psychic gifts, later these abilities were often viewed with suspicion. During the Middle Ages, people suspected of having divine or supernatural powers were accused of being witches or devil worshipers. Many of these people were arrested, tortured, and executed for their powers. These persecutions continued throughout the centuries, as evidenced by the trials and executions of witches during Colonial times in America.

During the past two hundred years, many psychics have become celebrities. Instead of being persecuted, people claiming or exhibiting signs of supernatural powers are sought out by a public eager for answers about the unknown. Today, psychics write their predictions in newspapers and magazines or perform on television to millions of eager viewers. There are even psychics who charge a fee for answering questions over the phone.

Those who claim to have special gifts answer a need for people who find comfort and security through the spiritual world. Hearing predictions from those who allegedly have a psychic or spiritual gift allows these people to feel closer to their god and have a better understanding of what their life may hold. In addition, most people have a natural curiosity about what the future holds and what will happen to them, their loved ones, and the world in which they live.

Not everyone thinks that psychic abilities are genuine. People who do not believe are called skeptics. Skeptics say that mystical or psychic abilities cannot be proven, or that they do not obey the laws of science. For this reason, they argue that supernatural powers do not exist.

Over the years, many people have claimed to have supernatural powers when they really did not. They may do this to achieve fame or to earn money. Some of these people might have some unusual gifts, but exaggerate them to make their powers seem more advanced. Others deliberately set out to trick the public to enrich themselves. These people and their actions provide even more evidence to skeptics that psychic powers are only make-believe.

Although most claims of psychic ability are probably not true, there have been a few people throughout history who seem to have been genuinely gifted. Some of these people, such as Hildegard of Bingen and Padre Pio, were members of religious orders who experienced visions or physical manifestations thought to have come from God. There's the world-famous sixteenth-century physician Nostradamus and pop psychic Jeane

Dixon, author of seven books, including an astrological cookbook and a horoscope book for dogs. Others, such as Edgar Cayce and Peter Hurkos, were believed to have used psychic abilities to help others through healing or solving crimes.

These mystics and psychics have become an important part of history. Their work, as well as people's reaction to it, shows a great deal about society and human nature. Whether people believe in their abilities or not, studying their lives gives society a glimpse into the unknown and provides a new way of looking at what might lie beyond ordinary sight.

An artist's impression of Hildegard of Bingen,
German nun, mystic, composer, and writer

Chapter
1

Hildegard of Bingen
MEDIEVAL MYSTIC

Hildegard of Bingen lived in the Middle Ages, at a time when women had little power or influence. Yet she became one of the most respected women of her age, and someone who was consulted by leaders of the medieval church. Much of her greatness and powerful reputation stemmed from a series of visions that she thought came directly from God. Hildegard's visions showed her a better way to live. She incorporated them into a series of books that still influence us today.

Hildegard was born in 1098 in Spanheim, an important religious center. At that time, Spanheim was located in an area called the Rhineland. Today the Rhineland is part of Germany.

Hildegard's family was part of the noble class. Her father, Hildebert, was a knight who owned a large amount of land. Hildegard was the tenth child in her family. Not much is known about Hildegard's childhood, but it was probably similar to other girls in upper-class families. These children generally received little schooling and spent their days working at home and learning domestic chores such as sewing, cooking, and how to run a household.

A sickly child, Hildegard suffered from a mysterious illness that sometimes left her unable to see or walk, and endured headaches and other physical pain she described as overwhelming. She had her first vision when she was just three years old, and later described this vision as an incredibly dazzling light that filled her with a sense of knowledge and God's power.

Hildegard believed that she had had the gift of visions even before she was born. She later wrote: "In my early formation, as God breathed sustaining life into me in the uterus of my mother, he implanted this capacity for vision into my soul. . . . In the third year of my life I saw such light as shook my soul, but because of my infancy I could not speak to anyone about it . . . and from then until I was fifteen I saw many things of which I spoke most simply, but those who heard me wondered where it all came from."

As a child, Hildegard realized that others did not share her gift, so she tried to keep it secret. She later wrote: "I tried to find out from my nurse if she saw anything at all other than the usual external objects. And she answered, 'Nothing,' because she saw nothing like I did. Then I was seized with a great fear and did not dare to reveal this to anyone."

However, sometimes evidence of Hildegard's mystical powers slipped out. Once she foretold the color of a calf before it was born. Hildegard's visions troubled her. She later wrote to a friend that she had felt anxious her entire life, even when she was a child. Hiding her secret became a terrible burden. To make matters worse, Hildegard's visions often were accompanied by illness and intense pain. She suffered from headaches and sensitivity to light.

During the Middle Ages, it was traditional to give the tenth child to the church as a tithe, or gift. Her parents may also have decided that the church would provide the best life for their little girl, who was already showing signs of mystical powers. So when Hildegard was eight years old, her parents sent her to live with a holy woman named Jutta of Spanheim. Jutta was a noblewoman who had chosen to become an anchoress. An anchoress led a life that was largely shut off from the world. She usually lived in a tiny room attached to a church. This arrangement allowed the anchoress to follow religious services. A tiny window provided the only opening to the rest of the world. Food was passed through this window, and refuse taken out through it as well.

Hildegard received only a basic education from Jutta. She learned to read and write, and learned some basic Latin, which was the language of the church. She also studied religious matters with a monk named Volmar. Later, Volmar would become Hildegard's secretary and good friend. Although Hildegard longed for more education and always felt ignorant and inadequate in this respect, she was much more educated than most medieval women.

Music was also an important part of Hildegard's education. She probably learned to read and write music from the monks at the church. Benedictine services were filled with music, and Hildegard enjoyed hearing the melodies every day. This exposure to music also helped Hildegard develop her own knowledge of this art form.

Just as Hildegard's family had done, many noble families sent their daughters to Jutta to be educated. In time, the anchorage expanded and became a small convent that followed the Benedictine Rule. The Rule was a series of instructions for daily living set out by a Catholic saint named Benedict, who founded twelve communities for monks near Rome. The Rule dictated every aspect of daily life, including what to eat, how to dress, and when to pray.

A 1926 painting by Herman Nieg of Saint Benedict of Nursia writing the Benedictine Rule in Heiligenkreuz Abbey in Austria

Being in a convent meant that Jutta and Hildegard had much more contact with the world than most anchoresses. Along with academic and religious subjects, Jutta taught Hildegard how to be a leader. This knowledge would come in handy later in Hildegard's life.

When Hildegard was about fourteen years old, she became a Benedictine nun. She remained at St. Disibod, which by now had both a monastery for men and a convent for women. Hildegard lived a quiet life, embroidering, praying, singing, and performing daily chores necessary to keep the community running. Although she continued to have visions, she told no one except Jutta and Volmar about them. They, in turn, did not share the news with anyone else.

Over time, Hildegard assumed more important duties as she helped Jutta run the convent. The others at the convent began to look up to her as a leader. In 1136, when Hildegard was thirty-eight years old, Jutta died. Hildegard had always helped Jutta and had shown great leadership qualities. Because of this, the other nuns all agreed that Hildegard should be the new prioress, or head of the convent. Hildegard shouldered her new responsibilities, and life went on much as it had in the past.

Throughout her life, Hildegard continued to have visions. During a vision, Hildegard's eyes remained open and she stayed conscious. However, she was not conscious of the outside world and saw and heard only images that came from the vision itself. As she once wrote in a letter, "I do not perceive with thoughts of my heart nor by any medium of my five senses, but rather only in my soul, with open eyes, so that I never experience the unconsciousness of ecstasy, but, awake, I see this day and night."

Light was an important feature of Hildegard's visions, and she believed that this light transmitted God's words to her.

She wrote: "The light that I see thus is not spatial, but it is far, far brighter than a cloud that carries the sun. I can measure neither height nor length, nor breadth in it; and I call it the reflection of the living Light." The "living Light" meant God.

Hildegard believed that her knowledge and her visions came directly from God, and that God wanted her to tell others about her visions. In the past, she had always kept these strange experiences secret from everyone except Jutta and Volmar. This was a terrible emotional strain, and Hildegard believed it caused her to become physically ill.

Still, Hildegard was too embarrassed and afraid of her visions to follow God's call. She did not feel she was worthy of such personal contact with God. She wrote: "But although I heard and saw these things, because of doubt and low opinion of myself and because of diverse sayings of men, I refused for a long time a call to write, not out of stubbornness but out of humility."

Hildegard also worried about what others would think of her. Since she was an important and respected woman in her community, revealing that she had visions might make people lose respect for her. She may also have been afraid of how the Church would respond to her. At that time, women were held in much less esteem than men, and were expected to be submissive and obedient to men. Many church leaders feared that women who acted in nontraditional roles might gain the power to break free of their "proper" position in society. The ruling male clergy were so frightened of women finding a voice and obtaining power within the church that they were quick to accuse any outspoken woman of suffering from hysteria or, even worse, of being a witch. Throughout history, the church taught that silence and humility were the only ways to honor God. For many years, Hildegard believed this and acted accordingly.

"The light that I see thus is not spatial, but it is far, far brighter than a cloud that carries the sun. I can measure neither height nor length, nor breadth in it; and I call it the reflection of the living Light."

At about age forty-three, Hildegard's outlook changed when she had a vision that was much more powerful than previous ones. She later wrote: "And it came to pass . . . when I was 42 years and 7 months old, that the heavens were opened and a blinding light of exceptional brilliance flowed through my entire brain. And so it kindled my whole heart and breast like a flame, not burning but warming."

This light seemed to fill Hildegard with a knowledge she had never possessed before. Now she believed she understood the exact meaning of the words of the Old Testament and New Testament in the Bible.

Hildegard came to believe that her mystical experiences, if shared with others, could provide guidance and help save their souls. She decided to seek approval to speak of her visions from Church authorities. Hildegard consulted with the Benedictine priests and the local archbishop. She also wrote to Bernard of Clairvaux, one of the most well-known and respected monks of the time. Bernard contacted Pope Eugenius III and told him that Hildegard had visions in which God spoke to her. The pope respected Bernard's opinion and believed him completely. The pope was so excited by what he heard about Hildegard that he encouraged her "in the name of Christ and St. Peter to publish all that she had learned from the Holy Spirit."

Once she had official Church approval, Hildegard was willing to express her visions. For the next ten years, she worked on her first book, a collection of visions. Hildegard wrote down her visions, and her friend and secretary, Volmar, edited and copied them.

Hildegard's first collection was called *Scivias* or *Know the Ways of the Lord*. In it, Hildegard wrote in God's voice and described the instructions God had given to her regarding how religious communities should operate. *Scivias* condemned many things about the Church of that time. It criticized priests who were uneducated, behaved sinfully, and did not carry out their duties. Hildegard also wrote that God felt people joined religious communities for the wrong reasons. Hildegard criticized the Church itself, saying that it was wrong for Church authorities to build fancy cathedrals and use money for their own personal gain. Instead, Hildegard called on the church to return to simpler forms of worship.

She also felt it was wrong to force young children into a religious life, as her family had done to her. She wrote the words God had given her in her visions: "If you offer your child to Me . . . and that offering is against his will because you have not sought his consent to it, you have not acted rightly. . . . He will come before Me arid and fruitless in body and soul because of the captivity unjustly inflicted on him without his consent."

Scivias was published in Germany in 1151. Despite its criticisms of the Church, the book was welcomed as a fresh voice of change. Many of the clergy agreed that the Church had moved too far away from its beginnings and from what God wanted it to be. Hildegard became well-known among Church authorities. She became a celebrity in Germany and among the Church community. People began to come to her for advice and comfort. She also became friends with important church leaders and consulted with them about religious matters.

When she was fifty-two years old, Hildegard left St. Disibod's. She said God had told her to start a new community in Bingen, a town on the Rhine River. The move to Bingen created a controversy. The monks at St. Disibod's did not want Hildegard to leave their community. Her celebrity had brought attention to the convent and helped it financially, because many of the visitors left gifts to the community. The monks were understandably reluctant to lose the source of their income and fame.

Hildegard was stubborn and determined to leave St. Disibod's and start the community she believed God had commanded. To accomplish this, she came up with a plan to get what she wanted. Hildegard took to her bed and lay there, silent and still. She remained this way even when Abbot Kuno, the leader of the monks, tried unsuccessfully to lift her head or turn her body. Kuno was convinced that Hildegard was truly ill, and that her illness was a sign of God's displeasure that she had not been allowed to move. Unable to go against God's will, Abbot Kuno gave Hildegard permission to start a new community.

The new community was called St. Rupert's. It included a convent and a monastery that housed more than fifty people. As head of this community, Hildegard enjoyed a position of authority and financial independence that was very unusual for women at that time.

Besides writing down her visions and running St. Rupert's, Hildegard was involved in many other activities. She also was a healer and an herbalist. Hildegard probably acquired knowledge of herbal remedies while working in the infirmary at St. Disibod's. Hildegard collected more than 2,000 remedies into books. Two major works, *Physica* (*Natural History*) and *Causae et Curae* (*Causes and Cures*), were published in the 1150s. These books contain listings of almost 1,000 plants and animals, along with medicinal uses for products made from them. In these works, Hildegard showed the importance of a balanced relationship between humans and the natural world.

Hildegard also believed that a person's diet and health strongly affected his or her mental state. She promoted a simple diet that is recognized today as being very healthy. Along with writing and medicine, one of Hildegard's biggest interests was music. She described it "as the means of recapturing the original joy and beauty of paradise." Hildegard firmly believed that music could restore balance in the world. Hildegard wrote the first known opera, as well as chants for women singers. Her music remains popular today among people who enjoy liturgical music.

One of Hildegard's most famous works was the *Symphonia*. This was a collection of chants intended for use during prayers and the Mass at St. Rupert's. The monastic day was built around prayers, psalms, lessons from Scripture, and music performed at seven specific hours during the day, plus a nightly prayer service called matins.

During these busy years, Hildegard began to write her second collection of visions. This book was called the *Liber vitae meritorum* or *The Book of Life's Merits*. In this book, which was written in 1158, Hildegard concentrated on encouraging people to live more holy lives.

Liber vitae meritorum described six visions focused on thirty-five vices, or sins. These vices included self-pity, greed, pride, and envy. Using knowledge gained from her visions, Hildegard describes the harm done by each vice, as well as penances or ways to receive forgiveness from God for these sins. The book is set up as a conversation between virtues and vices, and Hildegard uses different animals from her visions to symbolize each virtue and vice and show people how to live better lives.

As word of Hildegard's visions spread, people wanted to meet and talk to her to gain advice on how to live their lives or solve personal problems. Everyone from peasants to popes sought her out, believing she might have a personal connection with God.

Hildegard did not wait for people to come to her. She also journeyed to them. Between 1158 and 1160, Hildegard went on a lengthy journey, talking to monks throughout Germany. She would stand before the monks in the monastery's church or chapter house and give sermons that reprimanded lazy or misguided clergymen and advocated monastic and clerical reform. Hildegard completed three more of these speaking tours before the end of her life.

People were greatly affected by Hildegard, and crowds of men and women flocked to her from all over Germany. Many reported that her mystical powers allowed her to see into their minds and souls. Hildegard seemed to recognize what people wanted to say before they spoke. She also recognized people who were there to trick her or try to

Hildegard's Germany
Map Key
- • Settlement
- ⚨ Monastery
- ★ First Preaching Tour
- ▲ Second Preaching Tour
- ■ Third Preaching Tour
- + Fourth Preaching Tour

prove she was a fraud. Hildegard blessed the sick, counseled the troubled, and gave help to anyone who needed it.

Many people thought Hildegard had a direct link to God. Some even said she could perform miracles. A book written shortly after her death describes a situation in which a woman asked Hildegard to restore sight to her blind child:

"At one time, close to the town of Rudesheim, where she used to ford the currents of the Rhine and put in at a spot near the nuns' monastery, a certain woman approached her boat carrying a little child in the crook of her arms. She besought Hildegard in tears to lay her holy hands on the child. Being deeply moved . . . [Hildegard] drew water from the river with her left hand, and blessed it with her right. When she sprinkled it into the child's eyes, through the favor of God's grace it gained its sight."

Of course, not everyone viewed Hildegard as blessed by God. Some members of the church resented her criticisms and calls for reforms and called her a tool of the Devil. Others said she was crazy and accused her of trying to destroy the church. Hildegard had high-ranking friends in the Church, however, so she was allowed to carry on preaching, writing, and advising.

Many scientists think Hildegard's visions were actually the result of migraine headaches and have identified several features of migraines in Hildegard's visions. These features include seeing intense light, periods of blindness or paralysis, and a feeling of euphoria after the migraine had passed.

Hildegard continued to advise others until the end of her life. In 1171, when she was seventy-three years old, Hildegard went on her last speaking tour. Despite her age, which was quite old for the Middle Ages, she continued to write and run St. Rupert's, even though she lost a great friend and ally when her secretary,

Volmar, died in 1173. On September 17, 1179, Hildegard died. She was eighty-one years old.

In 1233, Pope Gregory IX began an effort to canonize Hildegard, or make her a saint. However, this effort did not succeed because of a lack of documented miracles. However, in 1324, Pope John XXII gave permission for people to worship Hildegard. Like the saints, Hildegard has a special feast day when people are encouraged to honor her and pray to her. Hildegard's feast day is celebrated in Germany on September 17. In 1979, Pope John Paul II celebrated the eight hundredth anniversary of Hildegard's death and called her "the light of her people and of her time."

Today, most of Hildegard's remains are in Rudesheim, near the Rhine River in Germany. However, her heart and tongue were removed and are kept as holy relics at Bingen, where her monastery still exists. Now it is called the Abbey of St. Hildegard, in tribute to a woman whose visions led her to create books filled with power and inspiration.

The Rhine River in Germany

The Benedictine Abbey of Saint Hildegard in Bingen, Germany

An 1846 painting of Michel de Nostredame, also known as Nostradamus, astrologer and physician

Chapter

2

Nostradamus
ASTROLOGER AND PSYCHIC

Nostradamus lived during the 1500s, a time when many people believed in astrology and psychic ability. As an astrologer and prophesier, Nostradamus won approval and support from the highest-ranking members of the French nobility. For centuries, scholars have studied his many strangely worded predictions, and some believe his prophecies have a connection to important historical events—even those that occurred hundreds of years after his death. The public's fascination with Nostradamus's work has made him perhaps the most famous psychic of all time.

Nostradamus's real name was Michel de Nostredame. He later changed it to Nostradamus, which is a Latin form of his French name. Michel was born in 1503 in Saint-Remy, France. His father, Jacques de Nostredame, was a grain merchant. Later he became a notary and town clerk, which were both important and respected positions. Michel's mother was named Reyniere, or Renee de Saint-Remy. Michel was the oldest child. Historical records are not clear, but it seems that Michel had seven or eight brothers and sisters.

The Nostredames were well-educated, well-respected, and wealthy. They were also of Jewish heritage, and Jews had been banned from France since 1394 because of vicious and long-standing anti-Semitism, or hatred of the Jews. Anti-Semitism had been common throughout Europe for many centuries. Jews were blamed for poisoning public wells, causing the spread of disease, and other horrors. The Catholic Church encouraged this hatred of the Jews, and some Christians did terrible things to Jewish people, including murder. To avoid the horrors of religious persecution, the Nostredames had converted to Catholicism years earlier. Despite this, they practiced the Jewish faith in secret.

Young Michel was especially close to his maternal great-grandfather, Jean de Saint-Remy. Saint-Remy had recognized that young Michel was very intelligent, and asked Michel's parents to allow him to raise the boy. The Nostredames were glad to give Michel this opportunity and allowed him to move in with Saint-Remy when the boy was quite young.

Saint-Remy taught Michel the basics of mathematics, Latin, Greek, and Hebrew. Saint-Remy was a physician who was also interested in astrology, or the belief that the positions of the stars and planets influenced people's lives. Saint-Remy passed his knowledge of astrology on to young Michel, and the boy's fascination with the stars became an important part of his life as an adult.

Jean de Saint-Remy died when Nostradamus was a teenager. Although there are no historical records of the incident, Nostradamus was certainly greatly affected by his great-grandfather's death. To continue his education, the young man was sent to the French city of Avignon to study at a Catholic school.

Nostradamus was an excellent student, but he was interested in some unusual topics, such as astrology. Although many people believed in astrology and it was considered a science in those days, it was still unusual for someone to show such a tremendous and obvious interest in it. The young man spent so much time talking about astrology that his classmates nicknamed him "the little astrologer."

Jacques de Nostredame was not happy with his son's interest in astrology. He thought his son's fascination was not practical, nor would it provide a good living for the young man. He decided that Michel should study medicine instead. In 1522, he sent nineteen-year-old Michel to the University of Montpellier, one of the best medical schools in France.

Studying medicine did not mean that Nostradamus had to give up his interest in astrology, however. At that time, astrology was an important part of medicine, and many people believed that the stars held power over a person's health and well-being. Nostradamus continued to study astrology as well as medicine and believed it was important to combine the two in order to truly be able to heal people.

By the age of twenty-two, Nostradamus had received his medical degree. He spent a short time teaching medicine in Montpellier. However, during the 1520s, a terrible disease called bubonic plague ravaged France and other parts of Europe.

BERNARD

A street near Nostradamus's home
in Saint-Remy de Provence, France

This disease was also known as "the Black Death" because of the black swellings that appeared on victims' bodies. The plague caused terrible suffering and was almost always fatal. Millions of people died of this disease during the Middle Ages.

Nostradamus felt compelled to use the knowledge he had gained in school and from his great-grandfather to help victims of the plague. He gave up teaching to travel around France to treat victims firsthand. Many of his treatments were unheard of at the time, and included plenty of fresh air and clean water. He also prescribed pills containing vitamin C. Nostradamus' remedies proved to be quite successful, and his skills made him a hero among the desperate French people. His treatments were certainly better than other prescriptions of the time. During the 1500s, harsh treatments such as blood-letting (draining blood from the body) were thought to be helpful, yet they actually made the patient weaker and less able to fight off disease.

Nostradamus took his treatments all over France. Soon he was credited with healing scores of people and delivering entire towns from the plague. His success increased his self-confidence and helped him remain strong in the face of devastating illness and death.

By 1534, the plague had run its course and was no longer a serious threat in France. That same year, Nostradamus married and settled down in the French city of Agen. Historians are not sure of the name of his wife, but one of Nostradamus's friends described her as being "of high estate, very beautiful, and very amiable." Soon, Nostradamus and his wife had a son and a daughter.

A few years later, disaster struck. Another plague struck the area, and Nostradamus's wife and children became ill. Nostradamus had been able to save so many people from this

Opposite page: This 1497 painting shows plague sufferers begging for God's mercy outside a church as the dead collect in the streets. During this time, many believed the plague was proof of God's displeasure with humanity.

dreaded disease, but he could not save his own family. Despite his best efforts, Nostradamus's wife and children died.

His family's deaths damaged Nostradamus's medical practice as well. His success in saving people from the plague in cities all over France was quickly forgotten. Few people had any faith in a doctor who could not save his own family.

Nostradamus's troubles did not end there. He got in serious trouble with the Catholic Church, which was the most powerful authority in Europe. The Church had established a court, or tribunal, to try cases of heresy. Anyone who spoke or acted against it faced arrest, torture, and even death. During this period, known as the Inquisition, people were often arrested by Church authorities on the mere suspicion of being against the Church or its teachings.

In 1538, Nostradamus saw someone casting a bronze image of the Virgin Mary and commented that the man was casting the statue of a devil. Shocked, the workman reported Nostradamus's words to Church authorities, who took the comment as an accusation that the Virgin Mary herself was a devil. Nostradamus insisted that he was commenting on the poor quality of the work. He also said that he was referring to the Ten Commandments and its instruction not to worship images of holy men and women. Whatever Nostradamus meant by his words, the Church was not happy with him. They summoned him to appear in court.

Nostradamus knew that such a summons could lead to torture or imprisonment. He decided to flee Agen rather than take his chances with Church authorities. Once again, Nostradamus became a wandering physician.

Nostradamus spent the next six years traveling through France and Italy, learning as much as he could about medicine and medicinal drugs. Historians believe Nostradamus met not only with other physicians, but with alchemists, astrologers, and magicians. Although little is known of his exact whereabouts during this time, reports of his prophesying began to surface.

One day, in 1553, he met a young priest named Felice Peretti on the road. As they passed, Nostradamus kneeled down to show respect. When Peretti asked him what he was doing, Nostradamus replied that he had to kneel down before "His Holiness," a title reserved for the pope. In 1585, many years after Nostradamus's death, Felice Peretti became Pope Sixtus V.

Nostradamus began to have a reputation as an astrologer and a prophet. When Nostradamus was invited to have dinner with a French nobleman named Monsieur de Florinville, his host decided to test him. As the two men walked around de Florinville's estate, they saw two pigs, one white and one black. De Florinville asked Nostradamus to predict which one they would eat that night. Nostradamus replied that they would eat the black pig, but a wolf would eat the white one. De Florinville then went to his cook in secret and told him to kill the white one and serve it for supper. While the pig was cooking, a young wolf that was being kept as a household pet came in and started to eat the white pig. The horrified cook quickly killed the black pig and served that animal instead. A seventeenth-century account of what followed reported:

"Monsieur de Florinville, believing he had won the day, knowing nothing of the accident which had occurred, said to Nostradamus, 'Well sir, we are now eating the white pig, and the wolf will not touch it here.' 'I do not believe it,' said Nostradamus; 'it is the black one which is on the table.' As soon as the cook was made to come in he confessed the accident."

Nostradamus's prediction and the strange turn of events quickly became the talk of the household.

In 1546, Nostradamus began to win back his good reputation as a physician. He was invited to Aix, France, to cure a particularly savage outbreak of the plague. This outbreak was so deadly that it was said that victims sewed themselves into burial shrouds when the first symptoms of the disease appeared. Nostradamus used his well-tested methods to stop the outbreak. The citizens were so grateful, they voted to pay him a pension.

The next year, Nostradamus moved to another town, Salon de Craux. There he met and married a rich widow named Anne Ponsarde. Nostradamus and his wife eventually had six children together. After his marriage, Nostradamus continued his travels, wandering from town to town to meet with doctors, pharmacists, alchemists, and astrologers.

After he settled in Salon, Nostradamus decided to devote more time to astrology. He also continued to prophesy about the future. He converted the top floor of his house into a study and filled it with books on the occult. He spent most of his time there, studying and prophesying. No one was allowed to disturb him.

Nostradamus had several ways of looking into the future. He placed a bowl of water and fragrant oils over a fire and stared at it to focus his thoughts. This process allowed his mind to open to visions of the future. He looked up past horoscopes and astrological charts and studied the positions of the stars. Then he used all this information to calculate dates and places where events would occur in the future.

By 1550, Nostradamus was writing and selling annual almanacs. Each almanac included astrological predictions and

An astrological sundial. Sundials are used to track the movement of the sun as a way of measuring time.

explanations of future events. The cover of one almanac read: "New PROGNOSTICATION and portentous prediction for the year 1555. Composed by Master Michel Nostradamus, Doctor in medicine, of Salon de Crau in Provence."

Nostradamus's almanacs were short works that came out every year. These almanacs became so popular that Nostradamus decided to write a longer work. In 1555, he published an ambitious project called *Centuries*. This book was a collection of quatrains, or four-lined rhymes. Each quatrain foretold an event that would occur in the future.

Centuries was not an easy book to read. The quatrains include scrambled words, and the book is written in several different languages. The rhymes include wordplay, puns, and anagrams. The predictions are not in chronological order, which makes it difficult to pinpoint specific dates when an event would occur. In addition, Nostradamus sometimes hid his subjects' identities in order to avoid personal or legal troubles in case his subjects weren't pleased about what he said. Nostradamus also created his book in this way in order to avoid specific accusations or claims that might be viewed as sacrilegious or connected with black magic. This was an important consideration given the power of the Church during that time and the feeling of many people that prophecy and magic were linked to the darker side of the supernatural.

The public enjoyed Nostradamus's book, and it attracted wide attention in France. Four years later, the book's popularity exploded because of the accidental death of King Henri II of France. Some people believe that this event was predicted in Century 1, Quatrain 35, which read:

> "The young Lion shall overcome the old On a warlike field in single combat, He will pierce his eyes in a cage of gold, one of two breakings, then he shall die a cruel death."

Initially, no one understood what this meant. But on July 1, 1559, when King Henri took part in a tournament that included a joust, the quatrain took on a new meaning for some people. In a joust, two knights on horseback ride toward each other and try to knock each other down using long, pointed weapons called lances. That day, Henri rode against a young man named Gabriel de Lorges, Comte de Montgomery. Their lances crashed together and splintered. Montgomery dropped his lance a second too late. The jagged point pierced the King's visor and entered behind his eye. The mortally wounded king fell from his horse. He died on July 10, after ten days of agony.

Many scholars have matched Nostradamus's quatrain to what happened on the field that day. The "young Lion" is Montgomery, and King Henri is "the old." The joust was the "warlike field in single combat." The "cage of gold" was the visor of Henri's helmet. Montgomery's shaft pierced the king's eye and broke into splinters in his brain, which is described by "one of two breakings." And King Henri did indeed "die a cruel death," since his injury was very painful.

Word spread of Nostradamus's prophecy. Some people thought the prophecy proved that Nostradamus was under the devil's power, since the power of prophecy was believed to be supernatural. A straw figure of Nostradamus was burned in Salon, and stones were thrown at his house.

The French court, however, saw Nostradamus's powers as a gift rather than an evil. After King Henri died, Francois II

King Henri II of France by painter
Léonard Limosin, circa 1555-60

became the next king of France. Francois was a sickly teenager, whose mother was Catherine de Medici. Queen Catherine was fascinated with Nostradamus and his prophecies. She believed that Nostradamus could predict the future for herself and her son. Catherine made Nostradamus her personal astrologer, counselor, and physician. The queen often sent for Nostradamus, and he traveled frequently between his home in Salon and the royal court in Paris. He also updated his prophecies in new editions of *Centuries* published over the years.

Less than a year after King Henri's death, another event occurred that some believed was predicted in Nostradamus's writings. In November 1560, young Francois returned from a hunting trip complaining of terrible pain in his ear. Members of the court noticed a lump behind his ear. The lump turned out to be a tumor. Soon Francois was very sick. Nostradamus's 1560 almanac stated, "One most young will lose the monarchy because of an unexpected illness." King Francois died on December 6, just seven weeks before his seventeenth birthday.

Besides the prophecies of events that occurred during Nostradamus's life, many predictions in *Centuries* have been linked to events far in the future. One of the most famous was his prediction of the Great Fire of London, which destroyed a large part of the city in 1666. Nostradamus also foretold the rise and fall of dictators that some believe were Napoleon Bonaparte and Adolf Hitler.

Nostradamus continued to prophesy and publish his almanacs for the rest of his life. He also remained a favorite of the French court. Catherine de Medici considered him to be a close friend and trusted advisor and even came to Salon to visit him in 1564.

Nostradamus's health began to fail during the 1560s. He suffered from gout, a disease that causes the joints to swell, and dropsy, or the retention of water in the body. In 1564, he began using a cane to help him walk. By the end of 1565, he was quite ill. In a letter to a friend, Nostradamus wrote: "Why it should happen I do not know, but the day after Gaspar Flechamar, the civic dignitary from Augsburg, visited me, I became afflicted with such rheumatic pain in my hands that I was not able to supply him with his horoscope on the day that we had agreed. The pains grew worse and went from my hands to my right knee, then into my foot. It is now twenty-one days since I had a good night's sleep."

In June 1566, Nostradamus told friends and family that he would return from a visit to the king and then would be dead when relatives found him in the morning. A few weeks later, on July 1, Nostradamus returned from a trip to see King Charles IX in Paris. That night, he told a friend, "You will not find me alive at sunrise." The next morning, his family found his body, already cold, lying across a bench he used to get in and out of bed.

Nostradamus left behind his wife and six children. He had told people that he did not want to be disturbed by feet walking over his grave, so he was buried standing up in a wall of the Church of the Cordeliers in Salon. His bones were later reburied in Salon's other church, the Church of St. Laurent, where they remain today.

Although he has been dead for more than four hundred years, Nostradamus continues to fascinate people today. Scholars continue to debate whether Nostradamus predicted events that occurred during modern times, including the devastating AIDS epidemic, the 1991 Gulf War, the *Challenger* shuttle disaster, and the death of Princess Diana.

While many people believe he was a true prophet, others have the opposite opinion. Skeptic Robert Todd Carroll points out,

"His prophecies have a magical quality for those who study them: They are muddled and obscure before the predicted event, but become crystal clear after the event has occurred." Carroll also points out that people often attribute the prophecies to specific events even if the details don't fit exactly. For example, a quatrain that supposedly foretold the *Challenger* shuttle disaster of 1986 says, "From the human flock nine will be sent away." However, seven astronauts, not nine, were killed in the disaster.

Another Nostradamus expert, Peter Lemesurier, portrays Nostradamus as someone who used his supposed prophetic powers for personal gain. The seer gained financially from his prophecies, as well as becoming a favorite of the French court. Lemesurier notes: "Nostradamus was a clever businessman, a PR man who knew on which side his bread was buttered. He left his language as vague as possible to cover every eventuality."

Over the years, hundreds of books have been written about Nostradamus and *Centuries*. Scholars will probably never understand everything Nostradamus wrote, nor will they agree on whether his talent was genuine. He made more than 7,000 predictions, and his prophecies extend to the year 3797.

In 1557, Nostradamus wrote: "In life I am immortal, and in death even more so. After my death my name will live on throughout the world." That is one prediction Nostradamus got right.

Edgar Cayce, clairvoyant, psychic healer,
"sleeping prophet," and theorist on reincarnation

Chapter

3

Edgar Cayce
THE SLEEPING PROPHET

Edgar Cayce (pronounced CAY-see) was a poorly educated young man from rural America. Yet his mental powers seemed to allow him to tap into all aspects of time and space. The resulting visions appeared to show knowledge far beyond what his education had provided. Extensive documentation of his predictions made him one of the most well-known and fascinating psychics of all time.

Edgar Cayce was born on a farm near Hopkinsville, Kentucky, on March 18, 1877. Hopkinsville was a small city and the county seat of Christian County, Kentucky. Cayce's parents, Leslie and Carrie Cayce, were farmers.

Young Edgar was the second child in the family, but the first child, a girl, had died before her first birthday. Cayce's parents would have four more children: three girls who survived and a boy who died when he was only ten days old. The death of young children was very common during the 1800s, when there were few medicines to cure diseases that could be easily treated today.

Leslie Cayce described his son as "unusually fine looking, large brown eyes, fat rosy cheeks, very bright and cheerful expression showing joy and happiness in his very early life. He was very healthy, strong and active, and with his happy and cheerful disposition, even as a baby, was more interesting to be with than he was a care." Cayce had a childhood that was typical of most farm children of his day. He helped his family on the farm, doing chores such as feeding the animals and harvesting the crops. Many members of Cayce's extended family lived nearby, and Cayce spent time visiting his aunts and uncles and playing with his cousins.

Edgar Cayce was particularly close to his grandfather, Thomas Jefferson Cayce. The two played games and worked together around the farm. Cayce felt that his grandfather took him seriously because the older man was always willing to listen to Cayce and answer his questions. This was somewhat of an unusual attitude in those days, as children were often instructed to be "seen and not heard" and were expected to be quiet and obedient, no matter what.

Cayce did not have many years to share with his grandfather. On June 8, 1881, the older man drowned after his horse threw him into a pond. Cayce was only four years old and was present at the tragedy. He later recalled:

"I was possibly the only one who saw him go to his death. I had been riding behind him on the horse when he first entered the pond. He returned to the shore and let me off before entering the pond again. I saw the horse throw him, and as the girth broke he disappeared under the water."

The drowning death affected Cayce deeply. After that day, Cayce was deathly afraid of water. He also began to feel that his grandfather's spirit was still present nearby. He said he sometimes saw his dead grandfather in the barn. Cayce understood that his grandfather wasn't really there; in fact he noticed that he could see through his grandfather if he looked closely enough. However, his grandfather's presence seemed very real to him.

When Cayce was about six years old, he began seeing other people who were not there. Some of these people were children who played with him. These children always disappeared whenever an adult was present.

Cayce's parents did not take his visions seriously. They assumed Cayce had imaginary friends, as many young children do. Other relatives, however, were upset and believed he was making up stories to get attention. "I was reprimanded by different ones of the family as I grew up," Cayce later wrote. "This gradually made me ashamed of these experiences, even though to me they were very real. I remember being called 'curious' or 'different' when I only wanted to be let alone and thought of as any other boy of my age. I did not want to be different."

Like many families of that time, Cayce's family spent a great deal of time in church. Cayce's earliest memory was accompanying his mother to religious services. Religious revivals were very popular at that time. These revivals were held in churches or in large tents outside and featured songs, sermons, healing services, and testimonials from people whose lives had been touched by God. These religious experiences had a powerful influence on Cayce and helped lead him to a lifelong interest in the Bible.

When he was still a child, Cayce decided he would read the Bible from start to finish every year of his life. From then on he never went anyplace without his Bible, which he read every moment he could. The Bible became the most important thing in his life and took precedence over his schoolwork and chores at home.

When Cayce was thirteen years old, he was reading his Bible in the woods. Suddenly, he said he saw a beautiful woman standing in front of him. The woman spoke softly and clearly, in a voice that reminded Cayce of music. He believed he was seeing an angel. According to Cayce, the woman asked him what he wanted most in life. Cayce replied that he wanted to help others,

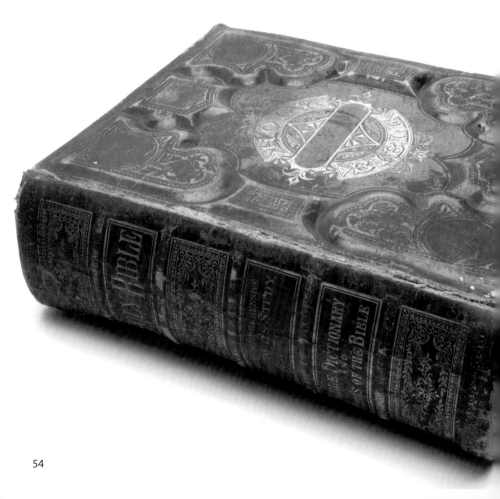

especially sick children. The woman told Cayce his wish would come true if he remained faithful and true to his beliefs.

Cayce's mysterious vision had a great affect on his school-work. The boy had attended several small schools, but his academic abilities were not impressive. It seemed that every time the teacher called on him, he was thinking about something else. No matter how hard he tried, he could not keep his mind on the lesson. Consequently, his parents and teachers considered him to be lazy and not very bright.

The day after Cayce had his mysterious vision, his performance in school improved dramatically. That night, he was going over spelling words with his father. The lesson was not going well, and Cayce asked his father to let him rest for a few minutes. He put his head down on his spelling book and fell asleep. When his father woke him, Cayce was able to spell all the words in the lesson. Even more astonishing, he could spell every word in the book. Cayce later discovered that he could sleep on any book, paper, or document, and photographically absorb its contents. From then on, Cayce slept on his books and had no trouble learning his lessons.

In spite of his new ability, Cayce did not remain in school much longer. After he finished the ninth grade at age sixteen, Cayce dropped out of school. The Cayces were having financial difficulties and he had to work to help support the family.

Cayce held a series of jobs over the next few years. First he went to work for his uncle on Cayce's grandmother's farm. Then, Cayce got a job at a bookstore in Hopkinsville, where his family had moved. Later he worked at a dry goods company.

By 1900, Cayce's father was running an insurance business. Cayce decided to join his father's agency as a traveling salesman. Cayce enjoyed the work and was quite good at it. During this time, Cayce also met a young woman named Gertrude. The two became friends, and then more than friends. Within a year, they were engaged, and planned to marry as soon as Cayce had saved some money.

One day in 1901, Cayce developed a terrible headache. A doctor gave him a strong sedative. When Cayce woke up the next day, he could only speak in a whisper. The severe laryngitis did not go away. Despite many different treatments, he spent the next year unable to speak except in a whisper.

Cayce could no longer work as a salesman because of his laryngitis. Instead, he found a job as a photographer's assistant. As he worked, he wondered if there was a reason for his laryngitis. He thought his voice may have been taken from him because it was meant to be the voice of a preacher, and he was being punished for not heeding the call to serve God.

Traveling entertainment shows were very popular during this era. As Cayce wondered how he might regain his voice, a traveling comedian and hypnotist known as Hart the Laugh King came to Hopkinsville to perform. Hart heard about Cayce's laryngitis and said he would cure the hoarseness for two hundred dollars. If Cayce was not cured, Hart would not take any money.

Cayce and Hart met in a doctor's office. Hart hypnotized Cayce and told him that he would be able to regain his voice. To everyone's amazement, Cayce was able to speak in a normal voice while he was hypnotized. However, Cayce's laryngitis returned as soon as he woke up. Although Hart tried several more times, he finally gave up and moved on to another town with his show.

People in the area were fascinated with the idea of hypnosis and had eagerly followed Hart's work with Cayce. The sessions were written up in several newspapers. A doctor in New York suggested that Cayce repeat the experiment, but have the hypnotist ask him to suggest a cure. Cayce found a local hypnotist named Al Layne, who also had some medical training. On March 31, 1901, Layne hypnotized Cayce and asked him to explain what was wrong with him and how he could be cured.

While he was hypnotized, Cayce said his illness was a psychological condition producing a physical effect. He also said that the condition could be cured by suggesting that the blood circulation increase to the affected areas. Layne made the suggestion, and he and Cayce's family watched in amazement as Edgar's throat turned hot and red. When Cayce finally woke up, he was able to speak normally for the first time in almost a year.

This cure marked Cayce's first psychic reading. Cayce used the word *psychic* to describe the incident because he thought that during a trance he was able to tap into paranormal powers to diagnose and cure physical problems. After Layne witnessed this, he asked for help for himself. Layne had been suffering from severe stomach pains, and he wanted Cayce to suggest a treatment. Cayce agreed. He put himself to sleep using a method he had developed, which involved lying down, closing his eyes, folding his hands across his stomach, and mentally commanding himself, step by step, to fall asleep.

Layne took notes of what Cayce said during his trance, including terms describing medical conditions and specific drug treatments. When he awoke, Cayce looked at the notes. "I've never heard of most of the names you have here," he told Layne. "I've never studied physiology, or biology, or chemistry, or anatomy. I've never even worked in a drugstore." Nevertheless, Layne used the medicines Cayce prescribed, and his stomach problems disappeared.

Layne wanted Cayce to go into business with him. Cayce could perform psychic readings, and Layne, because of his medical training, could carry out the treatments. Cayce was unsure, but finally agreed.

One of Cayce's earliest readings was for a five-year-old girl named Aime Dietrich. When she was two years old, Aime had gotten sick with influenza. Afterward, her mind had stopped developing, and she suffered from seizures. Cayce's reading indicated that Aime's condition was not just because of the influenza. A few days before she got sick, she had fallen and injured her back while getting out of a carriage. Cayce said that the influenza germs had settled in her spine. That was what was causing the seizures and brain damage.

Cayce suggested manipulative treatments to her spine, which Layne carried out. Within three months, the girl recovered completely. As news of the cure spread, more people came to Cayce and Layne for treatment.

Although Cayce was pleased to be helping people, he was uncomfortable when people said he was "special" and treated him differently. Cayce later wrote, "I felt decidedly embarrassed by what other people said to me and often I felt ashamed at being considered peculiar or different from others." Cayce especially did not want his readings to be the focus of his life. He just wanted to be a normal man with a job and a family. He especially wanted to marry Gertrude. On June 17, 1903, that dream finally came true, and he and Gertrude married. That same year, Cayce opened his own photography studio. A few years later, in 1907, he and Gertrude had a son. They named him Hugh Lynn Cayce.

Despite his desire to lead a normal, ordinary life, Cayce could not refuse people's requests for healing. The more psychic readings he did, the more famous he became. Stories about Cayce appeared in newspapers all over the country. In 1910, the

New York Times ran an article with the headline "Illiterate Man Becomes a Doctor When Hypnotized."

After the article appeared, Cayce received thousands of letters from people all over the country. Cayce said he could do successful readings on these patients even though he had never met them. He would simply lie down, put himself to sleep, and listen as his wife read a letter to him. Then he would dictate a course of treatment, sometimes using foreign languages and scientific terms he had never learned. The treatment was written down by a secretary, who later mailed it to the person who had asked for help. Cayce said he had no memory of what he said during a trance and had to read the transcripts to find out.

Cayce's fame grew, but he also suffered several personal tragedies during this time. In 1911, his younger son, Milton Porter Cayce, became seriously ill with whooping cough and a digestive condition called colitis. When Cayce gave a reading for his son, the diagnosis was that nothing could be done. Milton died before he was two months old.

Milton's death sent both Cayce and his wife into a state of depression. Cayce blamed himself for not performing a reading sooner, which could possibly have saved the boy's life. Things got worse when, shortly after Milton's death, Cayce's wife, Gertrude, became ill as well. Doctors said she had tuberculosis and would be dead by the end of the year. Cayce refused to give up hope. Instead, he gave a reading that recommended a combination of prescription drugs as well as filling a charred oak keg with apple brandy and having Gertrude inhale the fumes to clear up the congestion. Doctors claimed that the procedure would be useless, but after following Cayce's treatment for only two days, Gertrude's fever disappeared. Her health continued to improve, and by early January 1912, she was fully recovered.

Cayce also performed a psychic reading to heal his older son. In February 1913, Hugh Lynn was playing with flash powder in his father's photography studio, and seriously burned his eyes. The doctors said that not only would Hugh be blind, but one of his eyes was so badly damaged it needed to be removed. Instead of following the doctors' advice, Cayce gave a reading. This reading told him that Hugh had not completely lost his sight. Following Cayce's instructions, an additional compound was added to the medicine that had been prescribed by the doctors. Hugh Lynn remained in a dark room for two weeks with his eyes bandaged. When the bandages were removed, the boy could see. After newspapers in the area reported what had happened, Edgar Cayce's fame grew even more.

By 1923, Cayce was doing readings at least twice a day. However, he soon ran into a problem. He often prescribed specific drugs to restore the person's health, but many doctors refused to prescribe medications based on Cayce's advice. People also had trouble finding the herbal ingredients Cayce advised them to use.

Cayce realized that he needed a place where patients could obtain treatments based on his readings. In 1928, the Edgar Cayce Hospital opened in Virginia Beach, Virginia, where the family had moved in 1925. Cayce was able to found his hospital thanks to financial and business help from investors who believed strongly in his psychic readings. Although it was called a hospital, the organization was not a hospital in the traditional sense of the word, where sick and injured people went for emergency care. Instead, Cayce's hospital was a medical institution staffed by doctors who believed in Cayce's work and were willing to provide the drugs and treatments Cayce advised.

In time, Cayce gave readings on many different topics, such as advice about personal problems. He also answered questions about world events that would occur in the future, as well as where people might find lost belongings, or what they should do about a job offer. His readings covered the spiritual, mental, and physical health of hundreds of persons. For example, Cayce predicted the 1929 stock market crash and advised his friends to sell their stocks before it was too late. In 1931, he predicted several events that occurred during World War II (1939-1945). These glimpses into the future could be disturbing. Once, he left a room in tears because he recognized three young men from a reading he had done and felt he knew they would not be returning from the war.

On the other hand, Cayce's predictions were not always accurate. He said a huge earthquake would hit California between 1933 and 1936, and that Alabama would suffer a terrible flood between 1936 and 1938. The 1930s passed without either of these natural disasters. Cayce never commented publicly on his incorrect predictions.

Cayce believed that his ability was a gift from God and that during his sleep state, his mind traveled out of his body and came into contact with other places in time and space. He also believed that everyone was psychic to some degree. People often asked him how they could become more psychic. His response was always that they should become more spiritual. Cayce believed that if a person became more spiritual, he or she would be able to tap into their hidden psychic talents.

In order to help people use their psychic talents, Cayce and his backers founded Atlantic University in 1930. The school featured classes to help students understand and bring out psychic abilities, as well as classes focused on Cayce's theories about psychic abilities, reincarnation, and other supernatural subjects.

Despite Cayce's efforts, both the Edgar Cayce Hospital and Atlantic University were forced to close in 1931 because of the

The historic Cayce Hospital at the Association for
Research and Enlightenment in Virginia Beach, Virginia

economic hardships of the Great Depression. During this time, many people in the United States were unemployed and bank failures and a huge stock market crash wiped out people's financial savings. There was little support for experimental organizations such as Cayce's hospital and university.

Despite these economic hardships, Cayce and his friends were determined to spread knowledge from his readings to people around the world. In June 1931, Cayce founded the Association for Research and Enlightenment in Virginia Beach. The association was formed to research, investigate, and spread the information contained in Cayce's readings so that people around the world could learn about Cayce's methods and be helped by his psychic knowledge.

While performing psychic readings, Cayce learned a lot about people's experiences. This knowledge led him to believe that many of his patients had lived before. This is known as reincarnation, the belief that after death a person's soul is reborn into another life. Cayce wrote, "If a man dies, shall he live again? . . . I believe that when God breathed the breath of life into man, he became a living soul. The Spirit of God is life, whether in a blade of grass or in man. The soul of man is individual and lives on."

Cayce's belief in reincarnation was reflected in the work of the Association. Along with reincarnation, the Association studied many spiritual and psychic aspects of life, including holistic health care (viewing the body as a whole, rather than treating specific symptoms), extra-sensory perception (knowledge gained without using the ordinary senses of sight, hearing, etc.), meditation, spiritual healing, and the importance of dreams.

By the 1940s, Cayce was famous around the world, and was known to millions as "the sleeping prophet." He received sacks full of mail every day, begging for his guidance and predictions. Cayce felt an obligation to help these people. Even though his own personal readings advised him to give no more than two readings a day, Cayce began giving up to eight readings daily. His greatest ambition was to serve people. However, giving readings took a tremendous toll on Cayce's health and often left him exhausted and ill.

In 1944, Cayce became dangerously weak, possibly as a result of the emotional stress of his readings. In September 1944, he performed a reading on himself. The reading advised that he should rest until his health improved—or, until he died. Soon afterward, Cayce suffered a stroke and became partially paralyzed. He died on January 3, 1945. His wife died just three months later.

Gladys Davis had been Cayce's secretary for many years. After he died, Davis cataloged and indexed all the transcripts of his readings. The project took twenty-five years. When it was finally finished in 1971, the catalog included 14,000 readings on 10,000 different subjects. These readings are kept at the Association of Research and Enlightenment in Virginia Beach.

Edgar Cayce changed many lives. His influence lives on decades after his death thanks to dozens of books and hundreds of Web sites devoted to his work, as well as the efforts of the Association of Research and Enlightenment. He remains one of the best-known and most-studied psychics in history.

The Association for Research and Enlightenment Visitors Center in Virginia Beach, Virginia

Padre Pio, Italian priest, Catholic
saint, healer, stigmatic, and mystic

Chapter

4

Padre Pio

MARKED BY GOD

Padre Pio was a simple Italian priest who wanted to dedicate his life to Jesus Christ. Pio's intense devotion probably would have meant a life of quiet obscurity, except for one thing. He wanted to "be more like Christ," and events in his life indeed appeared to demonstrate amazing physical and mystical powers. Because of their belief in his abilities, millions around the world adored Padre Pio.

Francesco Forgione was born on May 25, 1887, in the small town of Pietrelcina, in southern Italy. Pietrelcina was one of the most desolate and isolated areas of the country. Francesco was the fourth of six children born to Grazio and Maria

Giuseppa Forgione. The Forgiones were poor peasants who worked the land. Their main crops were olives and wheat.

Like most Italian families of that time, the Forgiones were Roman Catholic. The family was deeply religious and spent much of their time in church. Francesco's father always carried a set of rosary beads so he could pray, even when he was working in the fields. The family home was decorated with a crucifix and other religious images. Young Francesco attended Mass, received the Catholic sacraments, and learned the story of his faith. From his earliest childhood, he was drawn to the religious life. His mother later described him: "Francesco never committed any fault; he was never unruly; he was a good boy and always obedient. Every morning and every evening he went to visit Jesus and the Madonna."

There were no schools in Pietrelcina, and most children worked in the fields instead of receiving an education. However, Francesco wanted to learn to read. Along with several other boys in the village, he spent evenings at the home of an educated farmer, who taught them in exchange for a small amount of money.

Grazio and Giuseppa knew that their son was interested in the religious life and wanted to get a better education. They found a private tutor for him, but lessons and books were expensive. To earn the money, Grazio immigrated to the United States and worked as a farm laborer in Pennsylvania. He sent enough money home for Francesco to get the equivalent of a high school education.

Francesco studied hard, but he spent most of his time in church. In addition to attending daily Mass with his mother or grandmother, he studied the lives of the saints with the parish priest. Francesco also volunteered to be an altar server and assist the priest during Mass. On feast days, he proudly marched in local parades to honor the saints.

Even as a child, Francesco yearned to be as much like Jesus as he possibly could. Two of the happiest moments of Francesco's life were when he received the sacraments of Holy Communion and Confirmation, because these sacraments made him feel as if Jesus was a part of him. (Communion commemorates the death of Jesus, and in a reenactment of the Last Supper, the words of Jesus—"This is my body" and "This is my blood"—are recited over bread and wine. The bread and wine are then shared by worshipers. During the Catholic rite of Confirmation a believer receives the Holy Spirit as part of their religious upbringing.) Francesco later wrote: "I wept because of the consolation I felt in my heart as a result of this sacred ceremony. . . . When I think of it, I feel completely ignited by that living flame which burns and consumes but causes no pain." The "living flame" meant Jesus.

It was clear that the young man had a vocation for the religious life. When he was ten years old, Francesco met a Capuchin friar named Fra Camillo. Fra Camillo was stationed at the friary of Morcone, about thirteen miles away from Pietrelcina, but he often traveled through the countryside. Francesco enjoyed spending time with Fra Camillo, who was fun-loving and kind. The boy was especially impressed by the monk's bushy beard, which was worn by all members of the Capuchin order. Once Francesco heard that, he told everyone he wanted to be "a friar with a beard."

As a youth, Francesco also had several mystical religious experiences. One of the most powerful occurred when he was fifteen years old. He was meditating on how difficult it would be to leave his home and family to study to be a priest. Suddenly, he saw a vision he described as "a majestic man of rare beauty,

A street in Pietrelcina, Italy

resplendent as the sun." The man told him he must fight a fierce warrior: a huge, dark giant. Francesco's companion promised to stay beside him and help him, and Francesco was able to defeat the giant. The young man understood that his guide was Jesus Christ, and his opponent was Satan, or the Devil.

On January 6, 1903, fifteen-year-old Francesco entered the Capuchin monastery at Morcone to study for the priesthood. It was traditional for candidates to the priesthood to choose a new name. Francesco chose Pio. He was called Fratello Pio, which means "Brother Pio."

Pio studied for seven years. The religious life was strict and difficult. Novices or students slept on hard beds and ate plain food. There was no central heating or air conditioning at the friary, so conditions could be quite uncomfortable. The novices spent hours in prayer and many more hours studying the lives of the saints, the rules of the liturgy, and the history of the Catholic Church and the Franciscan order. For most of the day, the novices could not speak to each other. Once, Pio's family came to see him, and found him standing with his head down and his arms folded. His family worried that he was ill, but Pio was simply following the rules of the order. It was only after Pio's superior gave him permission that he hugged his family and talked to them.

After several years of study, Fratello Pio was ordained as a Capuchin friar on August 10, 1910. With his ordination, the young man received the new name of Padre ("Father") Pio.

Padre Pio spent most of his priestly life at a Capuchin monastery in San Giovanni Rotondo. This small village was located in the mountains about two hundred miles south of Rome. In those days, it was impossible to reach the village except by a horse and cart. Here, Pio was truly isolated from the world.

Pio lived simply. His days were spent celebrating Mass, praying, and hearing confessions from people in the area. He ate and slept very little, and he wanted nothing more than to become closer to God. He was especially fascinated with Jesus Christ's suffering and death. When Jesus had been arrested and crucified, most of his followers had abandoned him. This abandonment greatly upset Pio, and he longed to be a faithful companion to Jesus, someone who would share his suffering and never abandon him. Pio wrote to a friend in 1910: "For some time I have felt the need to offer myself to the Lord as a victim for poor sinners. . . . This desire has grown continuously in my heart, until now it has become a powerful passion."

Pio's wish came true in a very unusual way. When Jesus was crucified, he received five wounds: one on each hand, one on each foot, and one in his side. These wounds are called the stigmata. In September 1910, about a month after he was ordained, Pio mysteriously received the stigmata on his own hands. He had sores about half an inch in diameter on both the front and back of both hands. Although the wounds did not bleed, they did seem to extend all the way through his hands. Pio described the experience: "Last night something happened which I can neither explain nor understand. In the middle of the palms of my hands a red mark appeared, about the size of a penny, accompanied by acute pain in the middle of the red marks. The pain was more pronounced in the middle of the left hand, so much so that I can still feel it."

The young priest did not want to draw attention to himself and was embarrassed by the stigmata. He prayed that the marks would go away, and he kept the marks a secret from everyone except the priest who served as his spiritual director. He told his spiritual director, "I do want to suffer, even to die of suffering, but all in secret." The stigmata disappeared a few weeks afterward.

A fresco (circa the early fourteenth century) by Giotto di Bondone depicting the moment when St. Francis of Assisi receives stigmata. Stigmata are bodily marks, sores, or sensations of pain resembling the five wounds Jesus Christ suffered when nailed to a cross. They are primarily associated with the Roman Catholic faith.

For eight years, Pio continued to serve as a priest. He also continued to pray for the ability to share in Jesus's suffering. Then, in 1918, the stigmata reappeared in a much more dramatic fashion. On September 20, Pio was praying before the crucifix at the Church of Our Lady of Grace, next to the Capuchin friary where he lived. Pio later wrote about what happened next:

"It all happened in a flash. . . . I saw before me a mysterious Person . . . his hands, feet, and side were dripping blood. The sight of Him frightened me: what I felt at that moment is indescribable. I thought I would die, and would have died if the Lord hadn't intervened and strengthened my heart which was about to burst out of my chest. The Person disappeared and I became aware that my hands, feet, and side were pierced and were dripping with blood."

Again, the appearance of the stigmata caused Pio embarrassment. When he had received the stigmata for the first time in 1910, he had been able to keep it a secret. Now that he had wounds that bled constantly, it was impossible to hide them, and Pio knew the stigmata would bring him unwanted attention. "I am dying of pain because of the wound and because of the resulting embarrassment which I feel deep within my soul," Pio wrote.

Padre Pio's stigmata caused more than embarrassment. The wounds were painful and bled constantly. He was forced to wear special bandage-like mittens on his hands at all times. Another priest later described them:

"The wounds in the hands were the size and shape of a coin. They were covered with a crust of dried blood. . . . The stigmata were very scary to look at. They were horrible to look at. . . . His hands were like those of a leper, they were so corroded."

Padre Pio also had wounds in his feet, which looked the same as the wounds in his hands. He also had a wound in his side that was reported to be shaped like a cross. All the wounds bled slightly but continuously. Sometimes the blood flow was heavier than others, such as during Lent—in Christianity, a time of fasting and repentance leading up to Easter, a religious observance that commemorates the resurrection of Jesus after his crucifixion.

Just as Pio had expected, people who had seen the stigmata began to talk about it, and word soon spread through San Giovanni Rotondo that something amazing had happened. People flocked to the monastery from miles around to see Pio for themselves. They wanted to meet this holy man and receive a blessing from someone who had apparently been touched by God. No one in the area had ever seen such a thing before.

The Catholic Church also heard about Pio's gift. The Church worried that people would begin to worship Pio himself because of his gifts. Worshiping a person is forbidden by the Catholic Church, which instructs that people should only worship God and His son, Jesus Christ.

Church authorities also worried that Padre Pio might be mentally ill and had inflicted the wounds himself. He might intend to fool others into thinking he had received this incredible spiritual gift in order to gain fame or respect.

To limit Pio's contact with and influence on the public, the Holy Office of the Pope in Rome ordered him to stop all public religious activities. Pio could no longer hear confessions, visit the sick, distribute Communion, or celebrate Mass in public. The Church hoped that these rulings would cause people to lose interest in Pio.

Although the restrictions were very painful to Pio, he bore them without complaining. He continued to live simply at the monastery, spending his days in prayer and meditations about Jesus.

During this time, several high-ranking Church authorities who believed that Pio's stigmata were genuine asked the pope to reconsider his restrictions. In 1933, Pope Pius XI sent two representatives to examine Padre Pio. These priests were impressed with him and told the pope he was a humble, genuinely holy man. As a result, on July 14, 1933, Pope Pius XI announced that Pio would once again be allowed to celebrate Mass in public.

A year later, Pope Pius XI allowed Pio to hear confessions. This was a great comfort to Padre Pio, as hearing confessions was an important part of his life. During confession, a person, or penitent, lists all the sins he or she has committed and asks for forgiveness. The priest who hears the confession instructs the penitent to say certain prayers or perform certain actions in order to be forgiven. Confession is a way for penitents to free themselves from sin and try to live a better life. Padre Pio felt hearing confessions was a way for him to set people on the road to God.

Padre Pio could hear up to twenty confessions an hour, which means he heard about a hundred confessions a day. Nothing unusual happened during most of these confessions. However, there are many accounts that describe Pio knowing what sins a person had committed before the penitent confessed them. One woman, Clarice Bruno, described how Padre Pio told her he would do all the talking, then proceeded to list the sins she had committed and offer advice for a problem she had not told him about.

Pio took the sacrament of confession very seriously and often scolded people who did not give the sacrament the proper

A Vatican photograph of Pope Pius XI taken after his election in 1922

reverence. Pio demanded that every confession be true and from the heart. He would not tolerate a lack of honesty in the sacrament of forgiveness. Pio even refused to absolve sins of penitents who were not sincere or who made excuses for their behavior. Although his treatment of insincere penitents could be harsh, he only wanted penitents to sincerely acknowledge their sins. Pio himself went to confession at least once a week.

Pio was a simple man who did not put on airs or look for attention. However, people were often overwhelmed when they met him and felt God's presence when they were with the friar. When noted Catholic author John Delaney met Padre Pio, he said it was "the nearest thing I could imagine to meeting Christ."

Many people reported smelling roses or beautiful perfume whenever Pio was around. Padre Pio never wore any aftershave or cologne, nor did he use scented soap. This mystical odor is known as "the odor of sanctity," according to the Catholic Church. It is considered another sign that someone is very holy and has a special connection with God.

Pio's celebrity status made it hard for him to go about his daily duties. He was besieged by crowds of people who came from all over the world and waited to see him in hopes of receiving a blessing. When Pio appeared in town, he had to be escorted by policemen because people would try to tear the clothes off his back and keep them as holy relics.

Part of the reason for this fervor was because Pio was credited with performing many miracles, including curing the sick. These reports, which were verified by church authorities, include a girl who had polio, but threw away her crutches and walked normally after Pio commanded her to; a seven-year-old girl who was born without pupils in her eyes and was totally blind until she and her grandmother asked Pio to heal her; and a man who could not bend his leg after a motorcycle accident but who was able to kneel down normally when he went to Pio for confession.

One of the best documented cases took place in 1949. A construction worker named Giovanni Savino had his face, including both eyes, severely damaged in a dynamite explosion while building an addition to the friary where Pio lived. Doctors believed that they could save his left eye but not the right. Savino's family asked the friar to help him. Shortly after midnight on February 25, 1949, Savino woke up and smelled the aroma of roses and felt a gentle tap on his right cheek. Later that morning, his bandages were removed. The young man's face was completely healed and he could see.

Over the years, Pio appeared to exhibit another mystical power, called bilocation, or the ability to be bodily in one place and spiritually in another place at the same time.

The first reported instance of Pio's bilocation occurred in 1918. One night, during a prayer meeting at the monastery, Pio appeared to fall into a deep sleep. Other priests tried to wake him without success. Finally, Pio awoke about an hour later. The next day, when a friend asked him where he had been, Pio answered that he was in America.

Sometimes Pio's bilocations were connected to miracles. In 1918, a friend of Pio's named Nina Campanile was worried about her very ill sister. Pio told her not to worry. That evening, Nina and a friend were sitting by the sick woman's bedside when the friend turned pale and said that she could sense Padre Pio's spirit in the room. A few minutes later, at eight o'clock, she told Nina that Pio had left. Then Nina's sister woke up, completely healed of her illness. The next day, Nina asked Pio if he had spiritually journeyed to her house. Pio replied that he had been there around eight o'clock.

Padre Carmelo Durante, a priest who was a friend of Pio's, recalled how Pio sometimes commented on his amazing abilities with a sly sense of humor. Durante explained:

"I was holding forth about a fact then unheard of: an aeroplane . . . had made the journey nonstop between Rome and New York in only six hours. To me and the others it seemed something incredible!

"The Padre who until then had kept silent, interrupted in the middle and asked: 'How long? How many hours did you say?'

"I answered with increasing marvel: 'Padre, six hours and what is more nonstop!'

"The Padre also marveled over the fact but to the side exclaimed: 'Six hours! Good heavens, but that is a long time! When I go it takes me only a second.'"

The most famous and celebrated appearance of Padre Pio's bilocation occurred during World War II. In 1943, while Italy was fighting against the Allied armies, San Giovanni Rotondo was targeted by American bombers. Several pilots said that when they appeared over the city and prepared to unload their bombs, a brown-robed friar appeared in the clouds before their aircraft. The soldiers tried twice to release the bombs, but the equipment did not work. However, not everyone believed this account. Father John D. Saint John, a chaplain with the Air Force division that supposedly tried to bomb San Giovanni Rotondo, said the incident never happened: "There was nothing in San Giovanni Rotondo at the time. There would be no point bombing it. . . . Someone must have been drunk and made up the story. . . . The story is impossible." However, other Air Force personnel vouched for the story.

One fact that cannot be disputed is that World War II extended Padre Pio's fame beyond Italy. Soldiers from the United States and Great Britain were stationed near San Giovanni Rotondo and heard stories about the mystical friar.

The Church of Santa Maria delle Grazie, or Holy Mary of Grace, in San Giovanni Rotondo, Italy.

Many attended his Sunday Masses and went to him for confession. After the soldiers returned home, they spread the word about this amazing man and the stigmata that marked his body.

As the years passed, Padre Pio's feelings about the marks changed dramatically. At first he was ashamed of them. Later, he thought of them as something that fortified his body and brought him closer to Jesus by allowing him to share Jesus's suffering. Pio came to love and cherish the marks, saying, "My wounds not only do not afflict my body, but they sustain and fortify it. I feel that what formerly depressed me, now invigorates me."

Writers have commented on Pio's extreme lifestyle. His intake of food was once estimated to be no more than an ounce a day. He also slept less than two hours a night. This, combined with the constant loss of blood from his stigmata, should have killed him. Instead, he remained frail but active throughout his life.

In 1968, Padre Pio's strength began to fail. On September 22, onlookers described him as tired and weak as he celebrated Mass and heard confessions for a large assembly of prayer groups devoted to him. While praying in his room at about 2:30 in the morning of September 23, he died. When his body

The body of Saint Pio of Pietrelcina in the crypt of the Church of Santa Maria delle Grazie

was viewed immediately after his death, the stigmata had disappeared completely.

People came from all over the world to attend Pio's funeral four days later, and the funeral procession was estimated to be almost five miles long. Like other members of the monastery in San Giovanni Rotondo, he was buried in the Church of Our Lady of Grace. However, Padre Pio's spiritual journey was not finished yet.

Padre Pio had many followers who wanted him canonized, or declared a saint. Just six weeks after his death, these followers began preparing detailed reports about his life. In 1983, the Holy Office began investigating Pio's life to determine if he was worthy of sainthood. Finally, in May 1999, Pope John Paul II beatified Pio. Beatification is the last step before canonization and allows the prospective saint to be called "Blessed."

June 16, 2002, was a day of great rejoicing for Catholics around the world. On that day, Padre Pio received the highest spiritual honor when he was canonized by Pope John Paul II.

A 1964 photograph of Peter Hurkos outside of a federal courthouse in New York City

Chapter

5

Peter Hurkos

PSYCHIC DETECTIVE

Peter Hurkos was an average man until he experienced a life-changing accident. The Dutch house painter fell off a ladder—and into a whole new world. After the accident, Hurkos claimed he developed amazing psychic abilities. He became known as a "psychic detective." He worked with police on a number of crimes and missing person cases, and also appeared on numerous television programs to demonstrate his abilities.

Pieter Cornelis van der Hurk was born on May 21, 1911. His hometown was Dordrecht, Holland. Van der Hurk's father was a house painter and a part-time opera singer. The van der Hurks were an ordinary middle-class family who worked hard and did not have much money. Van der Hurk's childhood was uneventful. He swam, rode his bicycle, played soccer, and roamed the woods around his home. He was also quiet and moody. His sister Allie recalled that "as a child, when he got upset he would run off to the woods or get in the little canoe and ride down the river and stay away for four or five days. He liked dark places. He didn't like to be with people."

Van der Hurk later said that he felt different from other children: "I was a black sheep from the beginning. I was a strange boy. I was born a strange boy. . . . Children didn't want to play with me when I was a kid."

Like most children in Holland, van der Hurk went to a local elementary school until he was fourteen. Then he went to a technical high school called Bankar Straas to study radio engineering. The course took seven years to complete. However, after only two years, van der Hurk had to leave school for financial reasons. He later explained,

> Upon leaving school, I went to work for my father. . . . He needed help with his work, but his business was not profitable enough to allow him to pay an outsider. . . . I left the gaiety and indolence of a boy's life to take on the responsibilities of a man. I had no inkling that I would not spend the rest of my life in much the same way my father had spent his. There was absolutely no history of extra-sensory perception, telepathy, or any other psychic awareness within my family."

During the spring and summer, van der Hurk painted houses with his father. During the winter, he worked as a cook on a ship that sailed from Holland to the South Pacific. During his second winter at sea, a stoker in the engine room got sick, and van der Hurk took over that job, which brought a welcome increase in his salary.

Being a stoker was hard work, but van der Hurk did not expect his work to change. Then, in 1930, the shipping company offered him a job in Shanghai, China, checking cargo and passengers. The job paid well, and van der Hurk enjoyed living in an exotic foreign country. But his time in China ended when World War II began in 1939. Japan occupied most of China during the war, and most European countries were at war with each other as well, so there was no more shipping trade between Holland and China. He returned to Holland, not sure what he would do next.

The war soon changed van der Hurk's life even more. On May 10, 1940, Nazi Germany invaded and occupied Holland. "Those few days in May changed all our lives completely," he recalled. "The Germans, once they occupied our country, were completely ruthless. They took our cheese, our butter, our eggs, our milk, our meat, our bread, and everything else of economic value to the German regime. . . . We Dutch were literally starving."

Appalled at the way his people were being treated, van der Hurk joined the Dutch resistance. The resistance was a group of people fighting in secret against the Nazis. They stole fuel and ammunition from German supply houses, smuggled people out of the country before the Nazis could arrest them, and passed along information that would help the Allied armies fight against Germany. If discovered, members of the resistance and their families could be arrested and sent to work camps in Germany, or even killed. To protect his family, van der Hurk changed his name. From then on, he was known as Peter Hurkos.

Along with his work for the resistance, Hurkos painted with his father. In June 1941, the two were painting a German barracks. Hurkos was standing on a ladder, and leaned over to reach a window. But the window was too far away, and Hurkos fell thirty feet to the ground. Hurkos later wrote about the fall:

" I remember this, how I hang over, and then I slip over and the ladder falls. And that moment I was falling, I saw my whole life pass before me, and I didn't want to die. I want to live. I was fighting, fighting, from the moment I was falling down from the ladder, because I didn't want to die. And then I fall down and everything was black."

Hurkos was rushed to Zuidwal Hospital, where doctors assessed his injuries. Hurkos had fractured his skull and suffered a severe concussion. He was in a coma for four days. Doctors thought he would die, or at least be seriously brain damaged.

When Hurkos woke up, he felt he was a different person. Later, he explained that while he was unconscious, he had a strange experience in which he felt a powerful light and heat all over his body. The light and heat grew stronger, drawing Hurkos into another world. There he saw nine important men from the past, who seemed to be gathered there to judge him. Hurkos later identified several of the men, including Galileo and Leonardo da Vinci. Hurkos said that the nine men talked about him. Then they told him his time on Earth was not finished yet, and when he woke up he would have a special gift. When Hurkos did wake from his coma, he said, he indeed had the ability to know things about the people around him—things about their past or future that were impossible for a stranger to know.

Soon after he awoke, a nurse came in to Hurkos's room. He grabbed her hand and told her she would lose her suitcase on the train. The nurse was shocked and told him she had lost her suitcase that morning on the train.

A few days later, Hurkos was talking to another patient who was about to be discharged. "He asked me how I was feeling, and after wishing me a speedy recovery, told me he was being released from the hospital after recovering from an emergency appendectomy," Hurkos later wrote. "As we shook hands and said goodby, in that instant I knew he was a British agent and that he was going to be killed by the Germans on Kalver Street a few days later. As the visions of his impending death raced through my mind, I unconsciously gripped his hand more firmly, shocked at the revelations, but not wanting to break contact. The stranger struggled to free his hand from mine and a look of terror crossed his face." A few days later, Hurkos read in the newspaper that the man had been shot and killed by the Germans.

Hurkos was released from the hospital four months after his accident. Hurkos found his new abilities very hard to live with. He was deeply disturbed by being able to know secrets about people just by touching them or touching objects that belonged to them. Sometimes he even thought he was crazy.

Hurkos became afraid to go out of the house because he did not want to talk to strangers and know secrets about them. But staying home was not much better. His family did not understand his new abilities or the change in his personality. Hurkos could not bear to be around strangers, but he was also uncomfortable in the presence of his family and friends. Hurkos had married a short time before his accident, but the marriage broke up under the strain of his strange new powers.

Employment was a problem too, because his visions affected his ability to concentrate. He later wrote:

> I could no longer work at anything I had ever done before. In acquiring my gift of insight, I had lost my power of normal concentration and attention. I could not keep my mind on one subject for more than ten or fifteen minutes. . . . For when I concentrated on any subject at all, the related visions of people and their associations kept creeping in. . . . They came as soon as I met a person or touched something that belonged to him, and they remained until I could divert my mind into another channel. Nor was it only people who disturbed me. I would pick up a coin, and if it had rested long enough in some person's possession, it would have a story to tell me. . . . Everything that had been touched by human hands could set me off."

This ability to know something about a person by touching an object that belonged to him or her is called psychometry.

Although Hurkos was never able to control his visions, in time he got used to them and managed to pick up the pieces of his life. He went back to work for the Dutch resistance. Not long afterward, Hurkos was arrested by the Nazis and sent to Buchenwald, a labor camp in Germany. Thousands of Jewish prisoners were killed by the Nazis at Buchenwald. However, Hurkos and other non-Jewish prisoners were kept in a separate part of the camp, where they labored for their Nazi captors. Hurkos was imprisoned at the camp for twelve months. He weighed a healthy 170 pounds when he entered Buchenwald, but weighed only 91 pounds when he was freed by American and Canadian soldiers. However, Hurkos considered himself lucky to have left the notorious death camp alive.

In May 1945, Germany surrendered, signaling the end of World War II in Europe. Hurkos returned to Holland, wondering

Dordrecht, Holland

how he would make a living since his psychic powers continued to disrupt his life. He decided the only thing to do was use his psychic gifts to make a living.

One day, a friend asked Hurkos to attend a show given by a psychic. Hurkos did not know that his friend had secretly sent a note to the psychic. During the show, the psychic took out the piece of paper, which said Hurkos was a better psychic. Amused, the psychic called an embarrassed Hurkos onto the stage. At the showman's prodding, Hurkos took the man's watch. Once he touched the watch, he was able to describe a lock of blond hair hidden inside the case. Hurkos also said that the hair was not from the man's wife, but from his girlfriend. Then, he pointed out the girl in the audience. The showman appeared surprised and embarrassed at this revelation.

Hurkos's performance caused a sensation as other members of the audience spread the word of the remarkable event. Word of the incident spread quickly. People began to ask Hurkos to give personal readings. He began to perform these readings to small groups in his home, charging a small fee for each reading. Each person would give Hurkos an object to hold and ask him a question. Hurkos would then tell them something about themselves or their family or friends that was connected to the object in his hand. Later, Hurkos also appeared before larger groups to raise money for charity. He identified personal problems for members of the audience and described events that had occurred in people's past or that would occur in the future.

By 1946, Hurkos had gotten the attention of a famous Dutch entertainer named Bernard Barens. Barens asked Hurkos to join his traveling show as a psychic, which featured a number of different acts. Hurkos enjoyed performing, but he felt his talent should be used for more important things. Soon he would find a way to use his unusual abilities to help people.

Early one morning, a woman who had heard the reports of Hurkos's psychic talents rang his doorbell. She asked for help to find her husband, who had recently disappeared.

Hurkos asked the woman to bring him something that belonged to her missing husband. The woman returned with a watch. When Hurkos held the watch, he saw a vision of the man taking a shortcut through the woods and falling through some ice. Sadly, he told the woman her husband was dead. The woman went to the police, but they did not believe Hurkos's story. The woman returned to the police station with Hurkos, and the two eventually convinced four policemen to go with them to a place called the Maljebaan in the Dutch city The Hague, where Peter said the body would be found. They found the dead man's cap in the bushes. Seven days later, the man's body was recovered from a water tank in the area.

Word of Hurkos's abilities spread among the police. Although they did not want the public to know, police departments around the world often talked to psychics in an attempt to solve difficult crimes. In 1947, the police in Limburg, Holland, asked Hurkos to help them solve the murder of a young coal miner named van Tossing. The man had been shot to death in his home, but police had no physical evidence to link anyone to the murder. Hurkos held van Tossing's coat and told the police the killer was a middle-aged man with a mustache, and that he also had a wooden leg and wore glasses.

The police said they already had a man in custody who fit Hurkos's description of the murderer. The man was Bernard van Tossing, the murdered man's stepfather. However, the police had no physical evidence to tie him to the crime. They hoped Hurkos could help them find something.

After handling objects belonging to the dead man and his accused killer, Hurkos had a vision of the crime. He told the police to look for the murder weapon on the roof of the van Tossing house. The police did as instructed and found a gun with two empty shells lying in the rain gutter. Tests showed that Bernard van Tossing's fingerprints were on the pistol, and he was eventually convicted of the murder and sentenced to life imprisonment.

Over the next three years, Hurkos worked on several other murders and missing person cases. His fame spread beyond Holland and all over Europe. In 1950, Hurkos was called on to help with his most notorious case yet.

On Christmas Day in 1950, the Stone of Scone was stolen from Westminster Abbey in London, England. The Stone of Scone is a huge rock that sits under the Coronation Chair, where every British monarch is crowned. It had been taken to London from Scotland more than six hundred years earlier, a theft that still angered many Scottish people.

Many people, in England and other countries, urged Hurkos to go to London and solve the mystery. When Hurkos arrived in England in January 1951, the police took him to the Abbey, where he picked up psychic impressions of the Stone's theft. Hurkos said that five men had been involved. He also drew a map of the route the robbers had taken from London to Glasgow, Scotland.

Hurkos told the police that the Stone had been stolen as a prank and would be back in Westminster Abbey in about four weeks. He also said it was hidden in the ruins of an old Scottish church.

Hurkos went back to Holland. Four weeks after its theft, the Stone was found in the ruins of an old church in Scotland. Five students admitted they took the Stone as a prank. The disappearance had been solved just as Hurkos had predicted.

In 1956, a professor and psychic investigator named Andrija Puharich invited Hurkos to come to the United States for a study. Dr. Puharich spent more than two years working with Hurkos in his Maine laboratory. He reported that Hurkos did indeed score better than average on tests measuring psychic abilities, and that he believed Hurkos was a genuine psychic.

Puharich's opinion was respected by some scientists and gave Hurkos credibility among the scientific and public community. Hurkos remained friendly with Dr. Puharich for many years. He also enjoyed living in America so much that he moved to the United States permanently after the research project was finished.

Hurkos's fame led him to work on several high-profile murder cases. Perhaps the most famous was the Boston Strangler murders. From 1962 to 1964, thirteen women were raped and strangled in Boston. The crimes terrorized the city.

Hurkos worked with Boston law enforcement on the case. One day, a police sergeant handed Hurkos a letter. Instead of reading it, Peter closed his eyes, and concentrated. Then he shouted that the man who had written the letter was the murderer. The man's name was Thomas O'Brien. Although Hurkos never met him, he accurately described O'Brien's physical appearance, the fact that he spoke with a French accent, and that he hated women.

Although police considered O'Brien to be a suspect in the Boston Strangler case, he was never charged. Instead, a man named Albert DeSalvo confessed to the murders and was sent to prison, where he was killed in a fight with another inmate several years later. Despite DeSalvo's confession and arrest, Hurkos remained convinced that O'Brien was the real killer. During the 1990s, many people came to agree with him. Recent evidence and forensic examinations have shown that DeSalvo did not kill at least some of the Boston Strangler's victims. It seems clear that either there was more than one killer or police arrested the wrong man.

However, not everyone believed that Hurkos had helped in the Boston Strangler case. One detective who worked on the investigation stated that Hurkos "contributed nothing to the investigation. . . . He did not contribute one thing to the solution of the Boston Strangler murders."

Albert DeSalvo taken into custody

Some members of the public felt that the police's credibility suffered because they worked with Hurkos. Two private groups that paid for Hurkos's expenses during his time in Boston said that Hurkos was difficult to work with. It did not help that during the case, Hurkos was arrested for impersonating an FBI agent. Hurkos claimed that his arrest was politically motivated and that police departments usually refuse to give psychic detectives any credit for fear of public ridicule. His response only led many people to believe that he was a fraud.

In 1969, a citizens' group asked Hurkos to help police working on a serial murder case in Ann Arbor, Michigan. Seven young women had been killed near university campuses in the city, and fear was running high in the community that the killer would strike again. Hurkos arrived in Ann Arbor in late July. After looking at pictures of the murder scenes, Hurkos gave the police the name and physical description of a man to investigate. Later, Hurkos changed this description. Soon afterward, a man named John Norman Collins was arrested and charged with the crimes. He matched Hurkos's revised description.

Many people were skeptical of Hurkos's work on this case. Although he had been right about several details, including descriptions of the victims' bodies and details about where the bodies were found, skeptics noted that many details had been published in newspapers, and Hurkos could have found out the details just by reading about them. Crime writer Katherine Ramsland noted: "On July 14, before Hurkos arrived [in Ann Arbor], a reporter from the *Detroit Free Press* had gone to California where Hurkos lived with photos of the victims, a map of the area, and some articles of clothing that had belonged to the victims. He might have filled Hurkos in."

During the 1960s, Hurkos married again and had a daughter, and enjoyed a happy family life. During the 1970s and early

1980s, Hurkos appeared on numerous television programs to demonstrate his psychic abilities, and even played himself in several television shows and movies. He also performed in nightclubs and concert halls.

Outside his career as a professional psychic, Hurkos demonstrated more conventional talents. He created abstract paintings and exhibited his work at New York's Museum of Modern Art and in other museums. During his final years, he became more interested in living quietly and painting, and did not appear in the media as often as before.

Hurkos died on June 1, 1988, in Studio City, California. Throughout his life, and even after his death, people have debated whether Hurkos had genuine psychic abilities. Some feel that he exaggerated his abilities or misrepresented the facts in order to appear more credible. Henry Gordon, an investigator who spent a year studying Hurkos and his work with police for a book called *Psychic Sleuths*, says that Hurkos had a method of "insinuating himself into cases so that his name would be attached to a case, even if he did not help or was dead wrong. What mattered . . . was the publicity." Gordon did not believe Hurkos had any psychic ability. However, other writers do believe Hurkos's claims. Crime writer Ramsland states that Hurkos "did seem to see some things about people that he could not have known. The truth about Hurkos probably lies somewhere in the middle. He had an uncanny gift but he wasn't as good as he (or others) claimed."

Although some people doubt his abilities, Hurkos himself always insisted he was an honest man who did his best with the strange gift he had received. "When you have a gift, you don't have to be afraid to prove it," he once said. "Sometimes people try to trick me, but I touch their object . . . I see pictures in my mind about what is happening . . . then I tell them."

A 1973 photograph
of Jeane Dixon

Chapter

6

Jeane Dixon

A CONTROVERSIAL PSYCHIC

Jeane L. Dixon was one of the most well-known psychics of the twentieth century. During her lifetime, she was a media superstar, thanks to several uncanny predictions of the future that were published in newspaper columns and her books, including an astrological cookbook and a horoscope book for dogs. However, Dixon also made many more predictions that did not come true, making her one of the most controversial psychics of modern times.

Jeane Dixon was born Jeane Emma Pinckert to Emma Von Graffee and Frank Pinckert in Medford, Wisconsin, on January 3, 1918. Her father was a successful businessman in the lumber industry. Jeane had six brothers and sisters. When she was a child, her father moved the family to Santa Rosa, California. Later, the family lived in Los Angeles.

The Pinckerts were devout Catholics, and Jeane grew up with a strong belief in God. The family attended Mass regularly, prayed at home, and made God and his teachings the central part of their daily lives.

When Jeane was eight years old, her mother took her to a fortune-teller. The fortune-teller read her palms and said that Jeane would be very famous and that she had a gift for prophecy. She also gave Jeane a crystal ball and told her she would be able to see things in it. Jeane said she looked into the ball and saw "great waves of blue water, and somehow realized that I was seeing the bay in a far-off land from which the gypsy originally came. I described what I saw, and she said it was just as she remembered it." This was the first recorded appearance of Jeane's psychic power.

Jeane made predictions several times during her childhood. Once, when her father was on a business trip, she told her mother that he would return with a big black and white dog. A few days later, Frank Pinckert came home with a large black and white collie he had bought to surprise his children. Emma Pinckert believed in her daughter's talent, but she told Jeane that God had given her a special gift—and, she could only use it for good purposes.

As she got older, Jeane became interested in astrology, or the relationship of the stars to people's lives. Jeane saw a connection between astrology and God because she learned a great deal about astrology from a well-educated Jesuit priest who was a friend of the family. She came to believe that studying astrology

Opposite Page: A fifteenth-century painting of Anatomical Man from *Très Riches Heures du Duc de Berry* (*The Very Rich Hours of the Duke of Berry*), a medieval book of devotionals and prayers for each hour of the day and time of year, according to the ecclesiastical calendar. Commissioned by John, Duke of Berry, the painting shows the signs of the zodiac as they correspond to each part of the body.

was another way to understand God's will. "When astrology is assigned its proper role as an aid to our self-understanding and to a better appreciation of God's will for us, then it will complement our religion and not contradict it," she later wrote.

Jeane's childhood and teen years were typical of an upper-class, close-knit family of the time. She went to school, socialized with friends, and traveled with her family. In 1939, she married James L. Dixon, a family friend whom she had known since she was a child.

James was older than Jeane, who was just twenty-one years old when they married, and he had been married and divorced. "Although my parents were Catholics and Jimmy's father was a Methodist minister," Dixon said, "our families were good friends . . . I had secretly been in love with him since childhood. He married when I was only twelve years old, and it nearly broke my heart. No one knew this, least of all Jimmy. If they had, they would have regarded it merely as a schoolgirl crush."

James was a real estate executive. When the United States entered World War II in 1941, he was assigned by the War Department to handle real estate transactions for the government. His job involved locating and purchasing land for government use, such as building air bases or housing for soldiers. The couple moved to Washington, D.C., where Jeane Dixon would live for the rest of her life.

Dixon worked in her husband's real estate office. She also spent a lot of time volunteering to help the war effort. One of her activities was serving on the Home Hospitality Committee. This group of upper-class women provided recreation for servicemen who were stationed in Washington or recuperating from war injuries in one of the city's hospitals. Dixon entertained the soldiers by doing psychic readings for them. Her readings proved to be very popular, and her positive attitude helped many of the injured soldiers see that they had a future despite their disabilities.

Washington, D.C., and Capitol Hill

A strong believer in extrasensory perception, Dixon said visions sometimes just came to her and filled her with a feeling of peace and love. She also used astrology, a crystal ball, numerology, and mind reading, and she sometimes touched her subject to receive information. Dixon also claimed to receive visions in dreams and "vibrations," or intuitions, about the future from a deck of cards.

Because of her husband's work for the War Department and her own charity work with the Home Hospitality Committee, Dixon was well-known among politicians and important government figures. Word of Dixon's abilities soon reached high places, and she quickly became an influential Washington socialite. In November 1944, President Franklin Delano Roosevelt asked Dixon to come to the White House. Roosevelt had been president for twelve years and was guiding the nation through the final months of World War II. The stress of his job had affected his health.

Dixon later wrote that when she entered the president's office and shook his hand, she sensed that the weight of the world was pressing down on him. Roosevelt asked her how long he had to finish his work. Dixon touched the president's fingertips and told him he had no more than six months to live.

President Roosevelt died suddenly of a cerebral hemorrhage in April 1945, less than six months after his meeting with Dixon. Although Dixon's prediction of his death was not publicized at that time, she wrote of it in her autobiography.

Dixon always said that she believed her abilities were a gift from God. Several of her visions occurred while she was praying or in church. In 1952, for example, Dixon received a vision that would make her famous. She always attended Mass before going to work at her husband's office. That morning, in St. Matthew's

President Franklin Delano Roosevelt

Cathedral in Washington, she said she stood in front of a statue of the Virgin Mary. Later, Dixon wrote of the vision that came to her at that moment:

> Suddenly the White House appeared before me in dazzling brightness. Coming out of a haze, the numerals 1-9-6-0 formed above the roof. An ominous dark cloud appeared, covering the numbers, and dripped slowly onto the White House. . . . Then I looked down and saw a young man, tall and blue-eyed, crowned with a shock of thick brown hair, quietly standing in front of the main door. I was still staring at him when a voice came out of nowhere, telling me softly that this young man, a Democrat, to be seated as President in 1960, would be assassinated while in office. The vision faded . . . but it stayed with me until that fatal day in Dallas when it was fulfilled."

Dixon told many people about her vision. Reporters heard about her prediction and mentioned it in the newspapers. In 1956, her prediction was published in *Parade* magazine. No one took much notice, until the election results of 1960. John F. Kennedy, a young, brown-haired, blue-eyed Democrat was the new president of the United States. The media brought back Dixon's prediction and people wondered if her vision might actually come true.

On November 22, 1963, Dixon was having lunch with friends at the Mayflower Hotel in Washington, D.C. When one of her companions asked Dixon why she wasn't eating, she replied that she was too upset because of a feeling that something awful was about to happen to President John F. Kennedy. Soon after Dixon spoke, an orchestra playing at the restaurant stopped. The orchestra leader, Sidney Seidenman, knew Dixon and her companions. He came to Dixon's table and told the women that the president had been shot while driving through the streets of Dallas, Texas.

Then he left to find out more about the president's condition. Seidenman returned with good news: The president had been taken to the hospital and was expected to recover. Dixon, however, disagreed. She told her companions that the president was dead. And, within half an hour, the nation received the news that President Kennedy had died.

Perhaps because of her Washington connections and status among the capital's political elite, many of Dixon's predictions involved politicians and other national leaders. Reportedly, she predicted the assassination of Robert F. Kennedy, the younger brother of John F. Kennedy, on June 5, 1968, as well as that of civil-rights leader Martin Luther King Jr., on April 4, 1968. And, in 1962, she met Ronald Reagan and she claimed to have told him he would be president one day. He was elected in 1980.

Reagan's wife, Nancy, had been a strong believer in astrology since the 1950s. Dixon became Nancy's personal astrologer after they met in the 1960s. However, Dixon stopped working for the Reagans during the 1970s. Reportedly, Dixon told Nancy Reagan that her husband would not be elected president in 1976 and Nancy became so upset at this news that she refused to speak with Dixon again. Dixon's prediction turned out to be correct, as Ronald Reagan was not elected president until 1980.

Dixon's predictions were not limited to political figures. Late in 1961, she predicted that film star Marilyn Monroe would commit suicide. Monroe was found dead of a drug overdose nine months later, in August 1962. She also foretold a severe earthquake in Alaska in 1964. Another accurate prediction was that the Berlin Wall, which divided East and West Germany, would fall and that pieces of the Wall would be sold as souvenirs. The Berlin Wall came down in 1989.

Although Dixon is credited with many accurate predictions, she made many more predictions that never came true. For example, she said that China would start another world war in 1958, and that Russia would be the first country to land on the moon in 1965. Neither of these events ever happened. Dixon also predicted a cure for cancer by 1967, and peace in the Middle East by 2000. The world is still waiting for those two events, and skeptics often bring them up when casting doubts on Dixon's psychic abilities.

Dixon made several political mistakes as well. She said that Richard Nixon would be one of America's greatest presidents. Instead, his administration was plagued by scandal, and he was forced to resign in 1974. Dixon also saw a woman president of the United States during the 1980s. Although 1984 saw the first woman to run as vice president on a major-party ticket, no woman was elected to the office of president or vice president during the 1980s.

Although millions of people around the world believed Dixon's prophecies and hung on her every prediction, many people dismissed her as a fake. Skeptics pointed out that her 1952

prediction that John F. Kennedy would be elected president was not quite as dramatic or clear-cut as had been reported. The 1956 article in *Parade* magazine that had detailed Dixon's prediction actually said that the 1960 election would be won by a Democrat who would be assassinated or die in office.

Robert Todd Carroll, who has written extensively about psychics, points out that this prediction was "broad enough to be shoehorned to a variety of possible events." He added:

> The president, whose name is never mentioned, could be assassinated in his first or his second term. He could die during his first or second term. He could have had a serious illness during either his first or second term. Any assassination attempts in either his first or second term might well have been seen as hits. But. . . she didn't name Kennedy and didn't say for sure that he would be assassinated."

John Allen Paulos, a mathematician at Temple University in Pennsylvania, studied Dixon and her predictions. He came up with the phrase "the Jeane Dixon effect" to describe the tendency of the mass media to exaggerate a few correct predictions while forgetting or ignoring numerous incorrect predictions. Carroll agreed. "My impression is that the mass media has done little to

belittle her reputation and much to enhance it. . . . When one makes as many predictions as Dixon did, you are bound to be correct or sort of correct some of the time. Even a broken watch is correct twice a day."

Pointing out Dixon's mistakes became something of a popular sport in the American media. Every year, newspapers listed predictions that hadn't come true. Dixon never publicly reacted to comments doubting her psychic ability. She simply ignored them and continued to predict future events.

Some members of conservative Christian churches also had their doubts about Dixon. Although she called herself a devout Catholic who was guided by God, many Christians could not reconcile her religious beliefs with her belief in astrology. To these believers, astrology is not only un-Christian, it has ties with Satanism. But Dixon defended her beliefs in her book *Yesterday, Today, and Forever*. She wrote:

> Some of my friends consider this [astrology] to be a strange practice for a Roman Catholic. As I understand it, however, the Catholic church and many other religious bodies as well have never condemned the study of astrology. . . . I have never experienced any conflict between my faith and the guidance I receive from my church on the one hand and the knowledge I find in the stars on the other."

Along with her own writing, Dixon was featured in countless articles. She worked with Ruth Montgomery, a well-respected journalist in Washington, D.C., to write an annual column of predictions that was distributed to eight hundred newspapers around the world. Montgomery described Dixon's incredible popularity: "By the decade of the 1960s, Jeane had become so widely known that mail from Europe and Asia, addressed simply to 'Jeane Dixon, U.S.A.,' was promptly delivered to her door. My annual columns about her predictions were syndicated here and abroad, and each time one appeared Jeane and I both received an avalanche of mail from readers who wanted her to help solve their problems or simply to foretell their future."

On January 25, 1997, Dixon died of heart failure at a Washington hospital. She was seventy-nine years old. She left behind seven books and a reputation as one of the best-known psychics of modern times. The truth behind Dixon's predictions may be a mystery, but she remains a fascinating figure. And, her predictions are still out there:

"Detroit will manufacture air-cushion cars by 2016."

"A charismatic leader lauded as a peacemaker in the 2030s will be revealed as a military genius and dictator."

"China will invade Russia in 2025."

Timeline

Hildegard of Bingen: Medieval Mystic

1098   Born in Spanheim in the Rhineland (now Germany).

1101   Experiences her first vision of bright light.

1151   Publishes *Scivias*, the first of two collections of her visions.

1158   Publishes *Liber vitae merirtorum*, the second collection of her visions, and goes on the first of four speaking tours, delivering sermons around the Rhineland.

1179   Dies at St. Rupert's.

Nostradamus: Astrologer and Psychic

1503   Born in Saint-Remy, France.

1522   Attends medical school and studies astrology at the University of Montpellier.

1555   Publishes *Centuries*, a collection of predictions in quatrains.

1566   Dies in Salon, France.

Edgar Cayce: The Sleeping Prophet

1877   Born in Hopkinsville, Kentucky, on March 18.

1890   Sees his first vision and learns he can absorb information from books by sleeping on them.

1901   Discovers his ability to diagnose illnesses and prescribe treatments while under hypnosis.

1931   Founds the Association for Research and Enlightenment.

1945   Dies on January 3 in Virginia Beach, Virginia.

Padre Pio: Marked by God

1887   Born in Pietrelcina, Italy, on May 25.

1902   Believes he sees a vision of Jesus Christ.

1910   Ordained as a Capuchin friar; mysteriously receives the stigmata for the first time.

1918   Experiences his first bilocation and his second stigmata.

1943   Experiences bilocation during World War II, while Italy is fighting against Allied armies.

1968   Dies on September 23 in San Giovanni Rotondo, Italy.

Peter Hurkos: Psychic Detective

1911   Born in Dordrecht, Holland, on May 21.

1941   Experiences his first psychic vision during a coma and discovers he is able to perform psychometry.

1946   Joins Bernard Barens's traveling show as a psychic.

1950   Helps solve the mystery of the stolen Stone of Scone using his psychic abilities.

1988   Dies in Studio City, California, on June 1.

Jeane Dixon: A Controversial Psychic

1918   Born in Medford, Wisconsin, on January 3.

1926   Sees her first reported vision through a crystal ball.

1952   Predicts the assassination of President Kennedy.

1965   *A Gift of Prophecy: The Phenomenal Jeane Dixon* is published; written by syndicated columnist Ruth Montgomery, the book becomes a bestseller, with more than 3 million copies sold.

1997   Dies in Washington, D.C., on January 25.

Sources

Chapter One: Hildegard of Bingen: Medieval Mystic

p.18,   "In my early formation . . ." Krista Scott, "Hildegard of Bingen and the Re/Visionary Feminine," http://www. stumptuous.com/hildegard.html.

p. 18,   "I tried to find out . . ." Fiona Maddocks, *Hildegard of Bingen: The Woman of Her Age* (New York: Doubleday, 2001), 55.

p. 21,   "I do not perceive . . ." Ibid., 58.

p. 22,   "The light that I see . . ." Jane Bobko, ed., *Vision: The Life and Music of Hildegard von Bingen* (New York: Penguin Studio Books, 1995), 35.

p. 22,   "But although I heard . . ." Kristina Lerman, "The Life and Works of Hildegard von Bingen," http://www.fordham.edu/halsall/med/hildegarde.html.

p. 24,   "And it came to pass . . ." Ibid.

p. 24,   "in the name of Christ . . ." Scott, "Hildegard of Bingen and the Re/Visionary Feminine."

p. 25,   "If you offer your child . . ." Other Women's Voices, "Hildegard of Bingen (1098-1179)," http://home.infionline.net/~ddisse/hildegar.html.

p. 27,   "as the means of recapturing . . ." Maddocks, *Hildegard of Bingen*, 89-90.

p. 29,   "At one time . . ." Ibid., 221.

p. 30,   "the light of her people . . ." Marcia Ramos-e-Silva, "Saint Hildegard von Bingen," http://www.dermato.med. br/publicacoes/artigos/saint%20hildegard%20von%20 bingen.htm.

Chapter Two: Nostradamus: Astrologer and Psychic

p. 38,　"of high estate . . . " Edgar Leoni, *Nostradamus and His Prophecies* (New York: Bell Publishing Company, 1982), 19.

p. 41,　"Monsieur de Florinville . . ." Ibid, 21.

p. 44,　"New PROGNOSTICATION . . ." Ian Wilson, *Nostradamus: The Man Behind the Prophecies* (New York: St. Martin's Press, 2002), 63.

p. 45,　"The young Lion . . ." Francis X. King, *Nostradamus: Prophecies of the World's Greatest Seer* (New York: St. Martin's Press, 1994), 17.

p. 47　"One most young . . ." Wilson, *Nostradamus*, 148.

p. 48,　"Why it should happen . . ." Ibid., 220.

p. 48,　"You will not find me . . ." Leoni, *Nostradamus and His Prophecies*, 37.

p. 49,　"His prophecies have . . . " Robert Todd Carroll, "Nostradamus," The Skeptic's Dictionary, http://skepdic. com/nostrada.html.

p. 49,　"From the human flock . . ." Ibid.

p. 49,　"Nostradamus was a clever businessman . . ." Peter Lemesurier, "Did Nostradamus Predict WTC Disaster Or is It Another Cruel Hoax?," FarShores ParaNEWS, http://www.100megsfree4.com/farshores/pred.htm.

p. 49,　"In life I am immortal . . ." Wilson, *Nostradamus*, 233.

Chapter Three: Edgar Cayce: The Sleeping Prophet

p. 52, "unusually fine looking . . ." Edgar Cayce, *My Life as a Seer* (New York: St. Martin's Press, 1999), 1.

p.52-53, "I was possibly . . ." Ibid., 5.

p. 53, "I was reprimanded . . ." Ibid., 8.

p. 57, "I've never heard of . . ." Thomas Sugrue, *There is a River: The Story of Edgar Cayce* (Virginia Beach, Va.: A.R.E. Press, 1973), 109.

p. 58, "I felt decidedly embarrassed . . ." Cayce, *My Life as a Seer*, 61.

p. 64, "If a man dies . . ." Cayce, *My Life as a Seer*, 225.

Chapter Four: Padre Pio: Marked by God

p. 68, "Francesco never committed . . ." Gennaro Preziuso, *The Life of Padre Pio* (Staten Island, New York: Alba House, 2002), 9-10.

p. 69, "I wept because . . ." Ibid., 15-16.

p. 69, "a friar with a beard . . ." C. Bernard Ruffin, *Padre Pio: The True Story* (Huntington, Ind.: Our Sunday Visitor, Inc., 1991), 35.

p.69-70, "a majestic man . . ." Ibid., 40.

p. 72, "For some time . . ." Ibid., 78.

p. 72, "Last night something happened . . ." Augustine McGregor, "Padre Pio. The Mystic," http://www.ewtn.com/padrepio/mystic/stigmata.htm.

p. 72, "I do want to suffer . . ." Ruffin, *Padre Pio: The True Story*, 79.

p. 74, "It all happened . . ." McGregor, "Padre Pio. The Mystic," http://www.ewtn.com/padrepio/mystic/stigmata.htm.

p. 74, "I am dying of pain . . ." Ibid.

p.74-75, "The wounds in the hands . . ." Ruffin, *Padre Pio: The True Story,* 161.

p. 78,   "the nearest thing . . ." John Delaney, *Saints Are Now: Eight Portraits of Modern Sanctity* (Garden City, N.Y.: Doubleday & Company, 1981), 107.

p.79-80, "I was holding forth . . . " McGregor, "Padre Pio. The Mystic," http://www.ewtn.com/padrepio/mystic/bilocation.htm.

p. 80,   "There was nothing . . ." Ruffin, *Padre Pio: The True Story*, 252.

p. 81,   "My wounds not only . . ." McGregor, "Padre Pio. The Mystic," http://www.ewtn.com/padrepio/mystic/stigmata.htm.

Chapter Five: Peter Hurkos: Psychic Detective

p. 86,   "as a child . . ." Norma Lee Browning, *The Psychic World of Peter Hurkos* (Garden City, N.Y.: Doubleday & Company, 1970), 40.

p. 86,   "I was a black sheep . . ." Ibid., 35-36.

p. 86,   "Upon leaving school . . ." Peter Hurkos, *Psychic: The Story of Peter Hurkos* (Indianapolis: The Bobbs-Merrill Company, Inc., 1961), 26.

p. 87,   "Those few days in May . . ." Ibid., 28-29.

p. 88,   "I remember this . . ." Browning, *The Psychic World of Peter Hurkos*, 44-45.

p. 90,   "As we shook hands . . ." Hurkos, *Psychic*, 17.

p. 91,   "I could no longer work . . ." Ibid., 55-56.

p. 97,   "contributed nothing . . ." Arthur Lyons and Marcello Truzzi, *The Blue Sense: Psychic Detectives and Crime* (New York: Mysterious Press, 1991), 110.

p. 98,   "On July 14 . . ." Katherine Ramsland, "The Nightclub Psychic," Crime Library, truTV.com, http://www.crimelibrary.com/criminal_mind/forensics/psychics/9.html.

p.98-99, "insinuating himself . . ." Ibid.

p. 99,   "did seem to see . . ." Ibid.

p. 99,   "When you have a gift . . ." Stephany Hurkos, "Peter Hurkos-Biography," http://www.stephanyhurkos.com/ peter_biography.htm.

Chapter 6: Jeane Dixon: A Controversial Psychic

p. 102, "great waves of blue water . . ." Ruth Montgomery, *A Gift of Prophecy: The Phenomenal Jeane Dixon* (New York: William Morrow and Company, 1965), 16.

p.102-03, "When astrology is assigned . . ." Jeane Dixon, *Yesterday, Today, and Forever* (Kansas City: Andrews and McMeel, 1990), 6.

p. 104, "Although my parents . . ." Montgomery, *A Gift of Prophecy: The Phenomenal Jeane Dixon*, 19.

p. 108, "Suddenly the White House . . ." Jeane Dixon, *My Life and Prophecies* (New York: William Morrow and Company, 1969), 18-19.

p. 110, "broad enough to be shoehorned . . ." Robert Todd Carroll, "Jeane Dixon," The Skeptic's Dictionary, http:// skepdic.com/dixon.html.

p. 112, "My impression . . ." Ibid.

p. 112, "Some of my friends . . ." "Astrology: Is It Harmless Fun or a Gateway Into the Occult?" http://www.biblestudy-site.com/astrol.htm.

p. 113, "By the decade . . . " Montgomery, *A Gift of Prophecy*, 121.

Bibliography

Bobko, Jane Bobko, ed. *Vision: The Life and Music of Hildegard von Bingen*. New York: Penguin Studio Books, 1995.

Brady, James. "Jeane Dixon May Have Been Wacky, But Divined Comedy Made Her a Star." *Crain's New York Business*, February 3, 1997.

Brian, Denis. *Jeane Dixon: The Witnesses*. Garden City, N.Y.: Doubleday & Company, 1970.

Browning, Norma Lee. *Peter Hurkos: I Have Many Lives*. Garden City, N.Y.: Doubleday & Company, 1976.

————. *The Psychic World of Peter Hurkos*. Garden City, N.Y.: Doubleday & Company, 1970.

Carter, Mary Ellen, and Harmon H. Bro. *Edgar Cayce: Modern Prophet*. New York: Gramercy Books, 1990.

Cayce, Edgar. *My Life as a Seer*. New York: St. Martin's Press, 1999.

Delaney, John. *Saints Are Now: Eight Portraits of Modern Sanctity*. Garden City, N.Y.: Doubleday & Company, 1981.

Dixon, Jeane. *My Life and Prophecies*. New York: William Morrow and Company, 1969.

————. *Yesterday, Today, and Forever*. Kansas City: Andrews and McMeel, 1990.

Flanagan, Sabina. *Secrets of God: Writings of Hildegard of Bingen*. Boston: Shambhala Publications, Inc., 1996.

Bibliography (continued)

Hart, Columba, and Jane Bishop. *Creation and Christ: The Wisdom of Hildegard of Bingen.* Mahwah, N.J.: Paulist Press, 1996.

Hurkos, Peter. *Psychic: The Story of Peter Hurkos.* Indianapolis: The Bobbs-Merrill Company, Inc., 1961.

Kalvelage, Francis Mary, ed. *Padre Pio the Wonder Worker.* New Bedford, Massachusetts: Franciscan Friars of the Immaculate, 1999.

King, Francis, and Stephen Skinner. *Nostradamus: Prophecies of the World's Greatest Seer.* New York: St. Martin's Press, 1994.

Leoni, Edgar. *Nostradamus and His Prophecies.* New York: Bell Publishing Company, 1982.

Lyons, Arthur, and Marcello Truzzi. *The Blue Sense: Psychic Detectives and Crime.* New York: Mysterious Press, 1991.

Maddocks, Fiona. *Hildegard of Bingen: The Woman of Her Age.* New York: Doubleday, 2001.

Montgomery, Ruth. *A Gift of Prophecy: The Phenomenal Jeane Dixon.* New York: William Morrow and Company, 1965.

Newman, Barbara Newman, ed. *Voice of the Living Light: Hildegard of Bingen and Her World.* Berkeley: University of California Press, 1998.

Preziuso, Gennaro. *The Life of Padre Pio.* Staten Island, New York: Alba House, 2002.

Ruffin, C. Bernard. *Padre Pio: The True Story.* Huntington, Ind.: Our Sunday Visitor, Inc., 1991.

Sugrue, Thomas. *There is a River: The Story of Edgar Cayce.* Virginia Beach, Va.: A.R.E. Press, 1973.

Wilson, Ian. *Nostradamus: The Man Behind the Prophecies.* New York: St. Martin's Press, 2002.

Web sites

http://www.newadvent.org/cathen/07351a.htm
Considered a saint by the Catholic Church, Hildegard's life is
chronicled here in an online article in the Catholic Encyclopedia.

http://www.hildegard.org/music/music.html
The music of Hildegard is explored on this site, in an article by
Dr. Nancy Fierro of Mount St. Mary's College in Los Angeles,
California.

http://www.nostradamususa.com
The Nostradamus Society of America provides a brief biography of Nostradamus, as well as a description of his prophecies.

http://www.padrepio.com
Includes information on Padre Pio and the Padre Pio of America
Foundation, which promotes devotion to him.

http://www.padrepiodevotions.org
Want to hear the voice of Padre Pio? Visit Padre Pio Devotions
of San Diego, a site that features the priest reciting the Lord's
Prayer and giving spiritual advice—in Italian. There's also an
extensive photo album.

http://www.edgarcayce.org
The official Web site of the Edgar Cayce Foundation features a
detailed biography of the psychic.

Web sites (continued)

http://www.cayce.com
A site devoted to health readings by Cayce. There's one on flu immunizations and fish oil to ward off diabetes.

http://www.forteantimes.com/features/articles/1520/psychi_in_
the_white_house.html
This link connects to the United Kingdom-based monthly magazine *Fortean Times,* which features a January 2009 article on Jeane Dixon titled "Psychic in the White House." The article is interesting and detailed and refutes many claims made by Dixon during her life, including her name, age, and how many siblings she actually had. Eight images also accompany the article, and, among other things, it reports that Dixon was connected to the FBI.

Index

Photo Credits

2-3: Courtesy of NASA
5: Used under license from shutterstock.com
7: Used under license from shutterstock.com
8-9: Used under license from iStockphoto.com
10: Used under license from iStockphoto.com
14-15: Used under license from iStockphoto.com
16: WoodyStock / Alamy
23: Used under license from iStockphoto.com
27: Used under license from iStockphoto.com
28: Courtesy of Sean Butcher & Carmen Butcher
30-31: Courtesy of Felix Koenig
31: Courtesy of Moguntiner
32: Réunion des Musées Nationaux / Art Resource, NY
36-37: Ian Dagnall / Alamy
39: World History Archive / Alamy
50: Mary Evans Picture Library / Alamy
54: Used under license from iStockphoto.com
56-57: Used under license from iStockphoto.com
59: Used under license from iStockphoto.com
62-63: Courtesy of Gingerkrick
65: Courtesy of The Association for Research and Enlightenment
66: Mary Evans Picture Library / Alamy
70: Svabo / Alamy
73 (bottom): Used under license from iStockphoto.com
80-81: Adam Eastland Italy / Alamy
82-83: Adam Eastland Italy / Alamy
84: Bettmann/CORBIS
88-89: Used under license from iStockphoto.com
92-93: Used under license from iStockphoto.com
99: Time & Life Pictures/Getty Images
100: Dennis Brack/Landov
104-105: Used under license from iStockphoto.com
107: Courtesy of Library of Congress
110-111: Courtesy of NASA
114-124: Courtesy of NASA

Book cover and interior design by Derrick Carroll Creative.